COLLECTED
ESSAYS OF
Jack
Holland

DEVORSS *Publications*

ISBN: 0-87516-685-7

Library of Congress Catalog Card No.: 95-70040

Printed in the United States of America

DeVorss & Company, *Publishers*
Box 550
Marina del Rey, CA 90294-0550

This book is affectionately dedicated to Dr. Jean Murphy, wife of the late Dr. Joseph Murphy, and to the Reverend J. Sig Paulson, both of whom have demonstrated faith in my work and have deeply inspired me.

Mentors of New Thought Series

Contents

Divine Energy

THE SUBJECT OF DIVINE ENERGY is, I am sure, of great topical interest, since everyone in the world seems to be talking about energy.

THE SO-CALLED ENERGY CRISIS

THIS IS NOT the first time in the history of the world that we have been faced with an energy crisis. During the last part of the nineteenth century a panic occurred because of a shortage of whale oil, which was the source of a vital type of energy. At that time of great fear, certain interesting people declared this fear to be ridiculous. If whale oil became unavailable, there were other sources of energy. For instance, Edison and Tesla began to work in the field of electricity; General Electric began developing an alternating current; and John D. Rockefeller, who was then but a small merchant, saw oil bubbling out of the ground and thought that there must be some new constructive use for that oil.

There are individuals today, too, who will solve our energy

problem, but the solution will not come through concepts of fear and limitation. These individuals will understand the wonderful nature of humankind in God. In finding the solution, I believe that the text of Job 28:28 will be of paramount importance: "The fear of the Lord is wisdom, and to turn from evil is understanding" (New English Bible). How we have misinterpreted the great knowledge in this statement!

"FEAR" OF THE LORD

IN THINKING OF THE concept of fear I like to use the acronym coined by Rev. J. Sig Paulson: "False Evidence Appearing Real—F.E.A.R." In fearing, we are so very often looking only at the outer appearance and ignoring the Divine source within. We should think of fear in regard to God as being something we delineate as awesome—full of wonder.

To "fear the Lord" is to know the Lord. The cultivation of a positive consciousness toward the Lord will solve all of our problems. This is wisdom. Wisdom is *not* the intellect, which is all the data we have stored. The intellect is sterile. Knowledge lifted up through love is real wisdom. "The fear of the Lord is wisdom, and to turn from evil is understanding." There is no evil in the world except negative ideas, and they come into manifestation, of course, in many ways. "In all thy getting, get understanding." Turning from the negative idea is understanding.

YOUR FRAME OF REFERENCE TO LIFE

WHAT IS YOUR FRAME of reference to life? Do you look at life as some kind of a mistake? No less an authority than physicist Wernher von Braun said that the odds against this earth and all the manifestations of energy having started with an accident are about five hundred billion to one. If our frame of reference is that everything happens by happenstance, that there is no place where we can turn, then we are developing the negative side and cultivating "the evil idea" as the authority in our lives. What is the authority in your life? Is it that there is no single Creative Force and Power? Is that the understanding you are cultivating? Is that your frame of reference? Then there will be no answers, and this Divine Energy, this Energy that can change all things, will be cut off from you.

WE ARE GOD'S TEMPLES

ACTUALLY, WE ARE GOD's temples, where the Spirit of God dwells. What does it mean to be "God's temple"? There are different levels of consciousness, and to enter the temple, consciousness has to be raised to a certain level. Most of us recognize that we have a tabernacle—where something within can grow—but many have never reached out to enter into the temple. The temple consciousness, of course, is the highest consciousness. To be God's temple means to be His highest expression. We really understand then that there is no limitation, that we are not cut off from His energy.

Jesus said, "I can of mine own self do nothing . . . the Father that dwelleth in me, he doeth the works." It is very important to realize that we do not do anything in our physical form alone, but that this temple of God can be lifted up through our acceptance, our cultivation, of our real nature. One of my favorite quotations from Ernest Holmes is: "We do not create energy, we distribute it. . . . So the will may decide what form the energy is to take but it cannot nor does it need to create the energy."* We are the releasers of energy, the middlemen, and

* *The Science of Mind*, p. 193.

we distribute it according to our consciousness, our awareness of what we are. We are God's agents, His stewards.

EVERYTHING IS HERE NOW

EINSTEIN WAS GREATLY influenced by the statement of Paul in Romans 8:19 (RSV): "The creation waits with eager longing for the revealing of the sons of God." Everything that ever will be or ever has been is here now, in essence, waiting for the revelation—waiting for us to lift our consciousness above its present level, which will bring in the new knowledge. For instance, was not electricity always here? Was not television always here? The missing element was an awareness of those things being here. This is why Paul said that things beyond our seeing, things beyond our imagining, are all prepared by those who believe (who cultivate the tabernacle, which becomes the temple of the living God).

BRINGING FORTH REAL ENERGY

CHARLES FILLMORE DEFINED energy as "the power of God within us to accomplish; strength or vigor of expression; internal or inherent power, as of the mind; capacity of acting, or producing an effect; power forcibly exerted; force or action; zeal in motion; the forerunner of every effect."* Energy has to be the forerunner of every effect. Bringing forth real energy, Divine Energy, requires the opening of the heart and mind to an awareness of what we are, of what we are a part of, and of the infinite nature of God as the Essence—the Omnipotence. God, the Creative Force and Power in the world, cannot create limitation. The Infinite *is* infinite; limitation has to be made, and it is made by

* *The Revealing Word*, pp. 62, 63.

a contraction of the mind. We make it through a limited consciousness of the Omnipresence. The doom-and-gloom people of our world are those with an absence of understanding of the nature of God. They are not aware that we are God's living expression, His temple.

REMOVE YOUR LIMITED AWARENESS

IN 1875 THE U.S. PATENT commissioner said that everything that could be invented had been invented. That was more than one hundred years ago! Fortunately, he resigned. With his consciousness, he did not belong in that job. But the point is, how many of us are resigning right now, surrendering to ideas of limitation—that there are no answers, that there is no constructive, creative ability in our world? We hear that there is nothing left to be discovered. Look at the word *discover*. It tells us the whole story. Dis-cover—remove the cover. We remove the limited awareness of what we are.

Throughout every period of history there have been thoughts of limitation, but, fortunately, there have been those who have come along and made themselves and others aware of the unlimited nature of God. We may be short right now of that which we have relied upon in a material way; but if we lift our consciousness, there will be new answers. Everything is already there for us.

THERE ARE NO IMPOSSIBLE PROBLEMS

THE "FATHER" OF our space program, Wernher von Braun, often said in regard to "impossible" problems: "Nonsense. Remember there is a perfect order in the universe and you and I can understand it." There is no such thing as an impossibility, only impossible attitudes, impossible current methods. All things are possible for those who believe. The amount of physical energy in our world today is exactly the same as it was at the beginning of time. Only form has changed. But so many of us are caught up in the form that we cannot and will not find answers.

A WONDERFUL OPPORTUNITY OPENS

AN ENERGY CRISIS opens a wonderful opportunity for the world, and particularly the United States, to demonstrate the potential in the unlimited nature of man. It is an opportunity to rededicate ourselves to the founding principle of this country, the realization of the uniqueness, yet indivisibility, of all human beings. This is the very foundation of the United States and, to me, an energy crisis is a great opportunity to re-express that principle.

IT IS GOD WHO DOES THE WORK

IT IS ESSENTIAL to recognize, as Jesus did, that it is God in us who does the work. This protects us. For as soon as we say, "I did it," we are "stuck" with whatever is currently in our consciousness. The ego runs away with us—becomes our death note. For it is through the recognition of God, infinite Wisdom and Abundance within, that one is brought into the awareness of limitless Divine Energy—the power for everything external and internal.

We must not forget that light, heat, and color cannot and do not exist through themselves. All physical energy, of many different forms, wavelengths, and vibrations, stems from the sun. The only physical light, heat, and color we can detect through our five senses are those which reflect off, or interact with, matter. Even in our sense-world consciousness, we are aware of the invisibility of most forms of energy. Has any of us ever seen an atom? Absolutely not. Has any of us ever seen an X-ray? An ether wave? A cosmic ray? Buckminster Fuller has said that approximately eighty-five percent of our work today in the scientific realm is in the area beyond the optical or hearing spectrums of humankind. Yet, when it comes to a practical problem today in the energy field, as we call it, we give up easily.

The entire process of life is a constant flux and regeneration of everything from the nebulae to the pebbles on the beach; and we tap into the very life process by recognizing the source. "The Father in me doeth the works." That is how we "get into" the life process. Yet, so many of us put the whole of our thought process, our whole "cultivation," on that which has come into material manifestation.

Again, the fear of the Lord—the cultivation of the consciousness of the one Presence and one Power, the I Am—is wisdom. It all depends, then, on our acceptance of our nature and of our own responsibility, our stewardship.

WE MUST LEARN TO ACCEPT OUR REAL NATURE

My discipline at San Jose State University for many years was Management. Undoubtedly, the outstanding writer and authority in this field is Dr. Peter Drucker, who is the founder of the principle of "management by objective and acceptance of personal responsibility." Management by objective without responsibility could be chaotic, and so could acceptance of personal responsibility without an objective. "Management by objective and acceptance of personal responsibility'' is exactly what Job was talking about in the Bible, in Job 28:28: ''Behold, the fear of the Lord, that is wisdom; and to depart from evil is understanding.'' The fear of the Lord, cultivation of consciousness of the Lord, of course, is management by objective; in this understanding, which is our responsibility, we achieve our freedom from limitation (evil). The stewardship of our nature is our personal responsibility. We must learn to accept our real nature, which is one with the Creative Force and Power. If we do not accept both the objective and the responsibility we are doomed to limitation.

RAISING OUR CONSCIOUSNESS

TODAY ACROSS THE WORLD we hear talk about the energy crisis. Divine Energy, the Source of all wisdom, knowledge, and freedom, is always there, waiting for us to ''plug in.'' Only we can cut ourselves off from this energy, and only we can ''plug ourselves in'' to it.

We all recognize, to a degree, that we have our very being through our oneness with the Infinite Mind. Whether we understand that life process or not is completely up to us—not to somebody else. As Jesus said, ''Pick up your cross [your understanding] and follow me.'' Each of us must carry his own understanding.

Because we exist through our consciousness, our cultivation of limited concepts and ideas will destroy us. But as we come into an awareness of our real nature, we become imbued with energy and alive to the infinite possibilities in life. We are designed—our world is designed—for perfection. In Truth, there is no energy shortage, no population over-expansion, no poverty, no illness, no limitation of any kind. God designed all for perfection. Our acceptance of this concept quickens us, energizes us.

We do not have to create energy, we simply distribute it. When we make it our will to know God, Divine Energy must automatically flow. "I am open and receptive to the will of God" is an affirmation widely used. "Thy will be done" in the Lord's Prayer opens the door to prosperity, peace, health, joy, and the overcoming of all seeming limitations. I deliberately use the word *seeming* because although there are limitations in the outer expression, that is not the truth of what *can* be there.

We distribute God's abundance through our consciousness of the Omnipresence. Our responsibility is to direct the power within. Every thought directs power. We are all directors. Learning to accept our directorship is what life is all about. We must realize that we are all one, and one with the Infinite Source of all. Since this is true, everything is ours and there can be no competition, no limitation, no shortages. Shortages are made, Abundance *is*; hate is made, Love *is*; illness is made, Health *is*.

ONE GREAT ENERGY

How DEPENDENT WE have become on electricity, which we brought forth by looking beyond the known into a new field of energy! All that electricity is, is a certain type of vibration. We have cultivated a real understanding of electricity, but let us lift up our understanding of the source of electricity and cultivate a knowledge of what this world is really all about. All emerges out of one great Energy.

The world has changed greatly over the past thousand years, and very rapidly in the past hundred years, through our knowledge of vibrations and energy. We have progressed from the discovery of energy from fire on down to the discovery of energy from the nucleus of the atom. Again, we must use this new discovery as good stewards. We are God's stewards.

Of those who feel that we are completely dependent on electricity, I would ask these questions: Was not electricity always there in potential? What is the ultimate source of electricity? Is it in the hydroplants, in the coal or petroleum being burned to produce it? And if this is the belief, what is there in the water power, the coal, or the oil that makes it possible for electricity to come forth?

THE POWER OF DIVINE ENERGY

JESUS KNEW HOW to honor the power of Divine Energy. He understood his own identity as the offspring of Spirit, with spiritual qualities such as love, wisdom, purity, and completeness. He was not intimidated by material forces, because he knew that he lived in the presence of the omnipotent Divine Spirit. Thus, Jesus was able to walk on the Sea of Galilee on a stormy night in complete defiance of gravity. He performed innumerable healing works, curing through Divine Power even the most stubborn ailments. He was a living witness of the biblical statement: "Power belongeth unto God" (Ps. 62:11).

We gain dominion over so-called physical forces through reliance on Divine Spirit. We must remember that we are the microcosm in the macrocosm, God, Divine Energy.

A LOVING DEMONSTRATION

WHEN I WAS a small boy, I showed my grandmother a cocoon of which I was especially proud. She said, "Why don't you protect and preseve this especially lovely cocoon? I will melt wax for you, and you can dip the cocoon in the wax and it will be preserved." Thinking this a good idea, I proceeded to "preserve" the cocoon by protecting the outer surface. Some weeks later, my grandmother asked how I liked having a permanent cocoon. I said, "Grandma, it is a nice cocoon, but the problem is that I can't release the butterfly, which should be beautiful.'' She said, ''Jack, this is why I had you preserve the cocoon. When we place our faith and trust on the outer surfaces (in the things of the world), the inner beauty and inner understanding are never released.''

What a great demonstration my grandmother provided for me! When we gaze only at the expressed world, no matter how beautiful it is, we never give our attention to the greater beauty, power and freedom which come only from within. Limitation always will appear in the expressed world until we come into the realization of our perfect state of oneness with the Omnipresence.

BECOME ATTUNED TO GOD'S PRESENCE

HAVING THE *knowing of God* as the chief objective in our lives, and accepting our responsibility to become *attuned to God's Presence*, we become conscious of and experience the Infinite. Through experiencing the Infinite, we dissolve all limitation and are living truly. We have our being in Divine Energy. When we understand our Source and how to relate to that Source, we shall be free of all limitation and there will be no more shortages of any kind. As Jesus said, ''Seek ye first the kingdom of God, and his righteousness; and all these things shall be added unto you.''

Patience: An Aspect of Healing

It is interesting that there is nothing in the scriptures more constantly referred to than patience—not always the word *patience* but the concept, the idea, of patience. Psychologically, patience is an important factor in mental health, and there is nothing in scripture that is more closely linked with love, the great and new commandment, than patience. Think about it: Why is this so? Why are we so often admonished to be patient? Think about the nature of patience. What is it, really? It is trust; it is faith. Obviously, patience requires an absolute trust, an absolute faith in an unlimited, unseen Power. Patience is the proof of the action of God in ourselves. It shows whether we have accepted in faith. *If we have no patience, we have no real faith.*

TIMELESSNESS IS THE NATURE OF GOD

Time does not exist in Divine Mind. It is very hard for one to realize that there is no such thing as time. Time is our

12

creation—not God's creation—because timelessness is the nature of God. There is no such thing as time in Divine Mind—there couldn't be. If there were, there would be limitation to the creative experience and potential. Time is a yardstick whereby we measure patience; but that very thing that is our yardstick for measuring is our creation. The word *time* comes from the Latin word *tempus*. Many of the things that come from the term *tempus* are very important to us in understanding impatience. Our word *temporary* comes from *tempus*—"time." Temporary is, again, our manifestation, because all that is form is temporary. It has to be temporary, because all things that we see in a manifested form are changing. There is no constancy in manifestation. So, again, we are measuring our concepts with a yardstick that really has no validity—not in reality. Our faith is tempted always in *terms of our patience*—whether we accept the limitlessness of God, which has no space and no time, or whether we have a limited idea of God, which has space and time.

"SPACE AND TIME ARE ONLY MAN'S IDEA"

I HAVE BEEN fortunate to have known Wernher von Braun, who, through his great work, got us to the moon, and who was the father of our space program. I can recall him always saying, "Remember that space and time are only man's idea." As we expand the horizons of our thoughts concerning our nature—in other words, develop a new faith—then, of course, space and time change. Have you ever thought of how you could possibly envision infinity? or eternity? There is no way that we could possibly hold a valid concept of eternity. Yet, there are so many who talk about going to heaven or about eternity. Heaven is not "there"—"there" is no such thing. It couldn't be. Eternity means the limitlessness of all. Of course, when we try to put God within a framework of time and space, we necessarily are limiting Him. As Emerson said, "To define God is to defile God," because it means we have to limit Him in our consciousness to a certain time-and-space spectrum.

Most of us pray and then we begin to worry: "Did God hear me?" "Will God answer?" "How can I check up to make certain I did it right?" "Can God do it?" So many of us make our prayers into a sort of divine billboard: "God, have you heard what happened to me today?" Infinite Mind, of course, knows all things. It knows what we need—like lilies of the field; the Father knows all of their needs. But we have this tremendous habit of praying and saying, "Yes, I trust God, but He's got to do it within 24 hours or else. . . ." We keep telling Him he has to be a kind of Divine bellhop. We try to bargain with Infinite Mind: "If You will do this for me, I will do that for You."

SUBSTANCE IS WHAT LIES BEHIND MANIFESTATION

ONE OF MY favorite stories is of Noah and the Ark. Noah and the Ark is a magnificent story about patience and developing faith. In that story, found in Genesis 6:16, Noah was told exactly how to build the Ark. Among other things, he was told: "A window shalt thou make to the Ark, and in a cubit shalt thou finish it above." Noah was told to make the window facing upward as a skylight; otherwise, those aboard might be running constantly to look out and to check up to see whether God was doing His good work. "The water is still rising!" "There is no land in sight!" "I don't see any birds flying around outside!" Obviously, their faith would be constantly undermined. Therefore, the Ark was built so that they would look upward all the time—not outward to see manifestation—looking upward so they would see reality, the truth of what really was. Many of us don't recognize that we are constantly undermining our chances for the fulfillment of the law of limitlessness and abundance because we are checking outward; we are looking at manifestation, and there is no substance there. Substance is what lies behind manifestation. Any physicist will tell you that.

I recently spent time with Dr. William Tiller, and this great physicist, who is the head of the Materiel Science Department at Stanford, said, "Isn't it interesting that we never could do anything in physics as long as we just dealt with the manifestation which man erroneously calls substance?" The story of Noah's Ark is a wonderful one because it tells us to look up; otherwise, we look out at that which has come into expression wherein there is great limitation. Can you not imagine what it would have been like on Noah's Ark if it had had windows or portholes? How each individual would have run to the window to see if his faith had been properly placed? Was God really keeping his Ark?

HAVE FAITH IN GOD

Ark is a very interesting word. Going back to the Hebrew meaning of *ark*, *covenant*, we find an ark is a chest or coffer to keep things sure or secret. If one kept opening it, nothing would be either sure or secret. The importance of the story of Noah's Ark is that we have an agreement with God—to have faith in God. That is what Noah did; he made an agreement with God. He came into an understanding (an agreement is an understanding) with God, and we, too, have an agreement—a covenant—with God. We must not keep checking up or there is no way for the completion to be sure and secret.

One of the most wonderful things that could happen to us would be to throw away our thermometers! Many of us will get out a thermometer every fifteen minutes when we are feeling ill and say, "Now, God, I've been praying, and I've been phon-

ing everybody and having everybody else praying for me; and
now I've got to check to see if you have really gone to work for
me." So, we take our temperature, and the temperature hasn't
gone down yet! God isn't listening! And up goes our temperature a little bit higher! It's a wonder we don't all die of taking
our temperatures! *Temperature* is a temporary thing: *tempus*
—time.

YOU CANNOT HAVE FAITH WITHOUT PATIENCE

ALL THAT THIS 'ark' means, of course, is that patience
is an absolute necessity of faith. *You cannot have faith and not
have patience. You cannot have patience without having faith.*
This is true in all respects—with no exceptions—whether it be
in the temporal state or the spiritual state. We must understand
that God works things out in His own time, which is limitless.
He knows the right time; but we keep undermining our faith by
putting in deadlines. They are deadly! They are *dead*-lines. They
are deadly to our consciousness.

As Jesus said, "Your faith has healed thee." Faith does not
exist for the healing presence without patience. Isaiah said, "In
quietness and confidence is your strength." The quietness and
confidence require tremendous faith, which is supported or destroyed by patience or the lack of it. In Divine Mind there is no
limit with regard to either space or time; hence, without patience we have to be working without faith. Don't we say in the
Lord's Prayer, "Thy will be done"? Then we turn right around
and say, "God, I give you 24 hours or I don't believe in you."
That's not faith! Faith is the understanding of the Presence always being present, no matter what the outer manifestation. As
we really come to recognize the wisdom of the fact that no one
knows the day or the hour of judgment, we develop patience. We

never know when a thought sown in the mind is going to erupt in the outer expression—any psychologist will tell us that. If we did know the time of judgment, we would not have all the psychologists disagreeing with one another.

I think it is interesting to watch some of our criminal cases and see how seven or eight eminent psychologists say a person is perfectly sane and seven or eight say he or she is absolutely insane! There is no science to it, but there would be if we recognized that no one knows the day or the hour of judgment—i.e., when the thought finally manifests into some*thing*. When we begin to understand that, as, of course, John understood it so well when he wrote the Revelation, we begin to strengthen our faith, and in so doing we strengthen our patience.

LIFTING OUR CONSCIOUSNESS

THERE IS NO way that we shall know the day or the hour. Our minds are limited to previous concepts, previous experiences, previous education. In other words, we are very limited in our ability to express ''limitlessness,'' and we are tied to concepts of space and time. The hour and day of judgment is whenever what we have sown through thought, deeply felt, manifests. That's the judgment. The day of judgment is upon us all the time, because every thought that we have deeply held, *every feeling that we have had*, we have absorbed into our very nature. When that absorption is going to affect us, we don't know. No one knows; but it will come forth. Infinite Mind, however, knows both the hour and the day for judgment—when it will manifest—whether it be the reaping of good, the healing, the purifying, or the reaping of evil. It will all depend upon what has been sown. The day of judgment must come upon us always —good and evil.

As we lift our consciousness to the truth of what we are, we develop more faith. Then the perfect expression will come forth at the proper time, in the proper place, and in the proper way. As we lift our consciousness to the awareness of God, trusting Him completely, we have the patience to allow God to flow through us and bring about His wonderful works. But it is faith and patience that allow God to manifest His will and His truth in us. Without patience (complete trust in God's will) we block the free flowing of God's energy and His radiance through us. Instead of becoming channels of expression for God, we become aliens to His perfect and abundant good. This is so important for us to recognize. It is the constant reaffirmation that nothing good has happened; it can't happen; it isn't working out right; my healing is not here; my good is not here; and constantly reaffirming and undermining the concepts that we have of God that block the perfect expression that is waiting for each and every one.

BRINGING THE PERFECT CONDITION INTO OUR LIVES

WE HAVE TO learn to become more as a thermostat and less as a thermometer. If we had a thermometer on a wall, that thermometer would simply recognize what is happening in the outer—it would be controlled by the outer environment. The temperature would go up or down in the thermometer by virtue of the manifestation in the outer. The thermometer is at the mercy of that which is already in expression. If we could become more as a thermostat, we could change from within and control the environment. There are things happening to us mentally, physically, and spiritually—all sorts of things—but we can, within ourselves, as a thermostat does, readjust through the knowledge of what we are; and we will then bring the perfect temperature, the perfect condition, into our lives.

Certainly, a thermostat has to register what is happening in the outer, but it pulls from the depths within and adjusts itself to the perfect key at which we set it. This is what we are constantly doing—we are setting a key by virtue of what we believe about the nature of God in ourselves. We are setting that key, and it is going up or down according to how we set that key. We would think it rather odd if we had a thermostat in our home and we kept going over to it and pushing it up and down. That is exactly what we do when we lack patience. We accept a certain level of faith in God, yet we keep going over there and pushing it up and down by undermining the nature of our belief in God. We must become more as a thermostat and less as a thermometer. We must recognize that the corrective power is within ourselves. As expressions of God, it *must* be within; we are not just registers of what has transpired in human-created space and time.

HUNGERING AND THIRSTING FOR GOD

IN GOD'S UNIVERSE there is no "empty space," nor are there any "time-limits." When we are impatient, we are trying to limit God to our concept of the "right" time and the "right" place. Impatience is an expression of no-God or a pagan God of limits in both spirit and matter. One of the most sustaining of all statements concerning patience is found in the Beatitude "Blessed is he who hungers and thirsts after righteousness for he shall be filled." It is the seeking for the right thought under all conditions, which is righteousness, which frees one from all limits of impatience. It is not the manifestation which one must seek, but rather the right "avenue"—"thought pattern"— which is to be desired. It doesn't matter what happens in the manifestation, because it will be fulfilling according to our hungering and thirsting. It is our hungering and thirsting for God that is all-important in determining the manifestation. The thought pattern is that which is to be desired.

So many of us wonder if we are really growing. We have a desire to better understand our nature—the nature of God within—and we wonder, "Am I really making any progress? Because I don't see it in my life yet; things are still going wrong, but I really want to see God, and I am hungering and thirsting, but I just don't see it in the manifestation." Don't be concerned about this. *The manifestation will come.* The fulfilling will come in the proper time and in the proper place according to God's law. It is the hungering and thirsting after righteousness which fulfills. "Seek ye first the Kingdom of Heaven and all shall be brought unto you." Patience is the key that frees us from time and space limitation. We must remember that the manifestation is the final thing—the judgment. It is the avenue to the manifestation—the quickening of the nature of coming alive to what we are—that makes the healing possible. That is patience —understanding the nature of God.

God has many times done His good and perfect work, and we upset the whole thing. We destroy everything He has done by not being patient, so we have to constantly reinforce our patience. We wait—not for the manifestation—but for our understanding of the nature of the God within. That is where it is —not the manifestation. Many in our world today hunger and thirst only after the manifestation, and so they lose sight of God. Hence, the hungering and thirsting become fruitless. The effective and freeing goal is gone.

UNDERSTANDING ULTIMATE REALITY

I LOVE WORDS, and one of my favorite is *salvation*. If you look it up in the dictionary, you will find that it comes from the same root as the word *salvage*, and it means to be free from the limitations of physical phenomena and coming to an understanding of ultimate reality. That's real salvation!

Healing requires great faith, and faith is manifested in large part by patience. As you develop a consciousness of the presence of God, you will have patience. With this consciousness of God's presence, there will be healing—there has to be. However, no man knows "the hour nor the day." So, don't limit God. See God in all things. Know that the Presence within you can overcome anything and everything. Don't try to be the judge. "Judgment is mine, saith the Lord." The time and the place is manifest through us in terms of patience—our faith and our patience. These are our handmaidens. Then we can say, as Jesus said, "Your faith has healed thee." It must be total and complete, but it is the hungering and thirsting after the right thought that makes it both total and complete. So, this *does* complete it.

We have to recognize that the manifestation is only that which is brought into form, and form is always limited and always changing. When we "leave" the manifestation and go to the cause (God), we will find our freedom from the limitations of time and space, the limitations that cause us to be impatient. "Seek ye first the kingdom of God" and you will have patience; through patience you will strengthen your faith and have your healing. Patience is the test of faith, and faith triumphant will heal all limitation. We now become one with the Creative Force and Power, and we become patient and obedient servants of the Father.

The Healing Image

How do you see yourself? When asked who you are, what is your immediate response? When questioned concerning you ambitions and your primary interests, what immediately comes to mind?

These are extremely important questions because how we see ourselves, who we believe we are, and what we make our ambition and our interests tell us whether we have a healing and perfect consciousness or not!

If we see ourselves as less than a perfect expression of God (Cause or Essence), believe we are only what we do as a vocation, or have as our first ambition and interest something that is manifested physically in the world, we are not in a consciousness which will bring healing, prosperity, and "enlightenment" to whatever our involvement is.

GIVING BIRTH TO THE
PERFECT HEALING IMAGE

ALL THINGS THAT are in manifested form and all ideas which are not God-oriented will *never* bring forth an ''image'' which will allow complete healing of the spiritual or the physical to take place. It is the understanding of the ''I Am That I Am'' which will give birth to the perfect healing image, and it is the only way that complete healing can ever take place.

If these sound like foolish statements, I would ask that you query yourself concerning how the doctor works with an individual who is ill. Would the physician ever apply medicine, perform surgery, or prescribe for the individual in any way if he did not know that truth was not in the disease or the condition that was being treated? Certainly not! The physician knows that the natural native state of the individual is perfect. He knows that all the medicine, the surgery, or the particular prescription does is assist in bringing forth the perfection (God) in the individual being treated.

It is the consciousness of the doctor and the patient that is all-important. When the doctor loses hope in the natural propensity of the body to work in harmony with all the laws of being, then he has lost sight of God in the individual. There is no such thing as a ''hopeless'' case—only a consciousness (either the doctor's or the patient's) of a lack of the Presence of God. Never believe anyone who says there is no hope. When this statement is made, the individual making it is simply stating that he does not understand the nature of God. In God and through God everything is possible. As Paul stated, ''Things beyond our seeing, things beyond our hearing, things beyond our imagination are all prepared for those who believe.'' With God as absolute Principle, with absolute power and absolute understanding, nothing is impossible.

WE ARE EXPRESSIONS OF GOD

Only in mind can we limit God. There is no other limit. A complete knowing that we are the image and likeness of God brings healing no matter what the outer demonstrates. We must remember that the "outer" is simply a reflection of our own thoughts. We cannot change, in depth, by looking to the outer (the manifested things of the world), because when we do we are simply seeing our own creation and not God's. It is through understanding ourself as an expression of God that the healing takes place: It is from within, out—not from without, in. The very meaning of education tells us much about this matter. Education comes from the Latin word *educare* and means to bring out from within. This is the type of education that allows us to develop the healing image; and it is the only type that frees us from the bondages of limitation in body, mind, and/or spirit.

Charles Fillmore states that the ability to merge our mind in the one Mind makes a great person of us. This is true, and it also makes for the healing image. When we know without any reservation whatsoever that we are expressions of God, then there can only be harmony, peace, joy, and health in our being. It is the doubting and the lack of faith in the Divine Presence in us that create the illusion of disharmony, chaos, unhappiness, and illness. When we know that we are expressions of God, there is simply nothing that we cannot overcome because we can activate the God Expression in us, and, with God, nothing is impossible.

Jesus told us very clearly exactly how to come into the healing image, the enlightenment image, the prosperity image, and the peaceful image. He said, "Be ye perfect even as your Father in Heaven." It would be impossible for an individual to become perfect unless we were an expression of that which is perfect. In perfection there can be nothing except that which is acceptable in the eyes of God, and that has to be complete health, complete joy, complete peace, and complete harmony.

OUR AUTHORITY BELIEF

SOME BELIEF IN a type of authority is always required to create any image. We always work in mind from some premise. Whatever the premise, the framework will be responsible for the image that emerges. What do we take as the final authority in our affairs? Is it the learned academician, the physician, the counselor, the psychic, the astrologer, or the soothsayer? Find what an individual establishes as the authority in his life and you will find the answer to why he has certain images in his world. Today, many accept as the "authority" in their lives only that which has been printed, enunciated over television or radio, or stated by some governmental, social, or fiscal expert. We are placing our authority (our frame of reference) on those things which are of the outer world, and there is nothing to draw from and nothing to provide sustenance when the authority develops "feet of clay" or is disproved. We are planting our authority (our faith) on very sandy foundations, and we are naturally caught up and maneuvered by every wind of adversity that comes along.

Again, Jesus told us so very clearly that our authority should be the same as His authority: "All authority hath been given unto me in heaven and on earth." Jesus knew of his Divine Sonship and accepted it in every way. He made it his ready reference, and it was his authority for all consciousness. Hence, he held the perfect image of what he was, and so he had the healing image. Paul wrote, "But if the Spirit of him that raised up Jesus from the dead dwelleth in you, he that raised up Christ Jesus from the dead shall give life also to your mortal bodies through his Spirit that dwelleth in you."

WITH GOD ALL THINGS
ARE POSSIBLE

IT IS THE recognition of God as First Cause, as the I Am Presence in ourselves, that will allow the healing image to become firm and permanent. But how difficult this is for most of us to do! Most of us look to the outer expressed manifestations for our substance and we see limitation, illness, and poverty. These things become our foundation and our "images" of the world. These impressions are lies and abominations. They exist, but they are not the Truth. They are limited expressions of Truth that are there because of the absence of God in consciousness. When we bring God into consciousness and know God as our Father, all of the limitations will go back to the nothingness from which they came. When we become God-worshipers, we will come into the image and likeness of God, which is our native nature. God created us like unto Himself and with God all things are possible—*all* things, with no exception whatsoever. If we begin to accept the Truth of the fact that we are in the image and likeness of God, then we have begun to build the healing image.

There is no limit to what God can do. Just as Jesus raised Lazarus from the dead, we, too, can raise everything that is limiting in our lives to the point where all things are perfect, all things are beautiful, and all things are of good report. However, to raise anything means to "lift up" from the present form or condition. Since everything begins in thought, the higher the thought the greater the "raising." When thoughts are turned to the I Am Presence, to the awareness of God within, the raising will be complete whether a raising of physical being, spiritual realization, or health. Having the image of God as the authority for living will bring the perfect life. An absence of His consciousness will have to produce various and assorted forms of limitation.

A HEALING MIRACLE

A DEAR FRIEND of mine was stricken with a serious illness when she was a very small girl. When she recovered from this severe illness, her left leg ceased growing. At full womanhood her left leg was more than four inches shorter than her right, and various manifestations of problems appeared in addition to the lack of limb development. She was treated by great and good physicians and surgeons to no avail. Although she loved to dance and had great native abilities along this line, dancing became virtually impossible for her. In her youth, women did not wear slacks, so there was the added burden of revealing what appeared to be a deformed leg. After she became a wife and mother, with the assistance of her father and many loved ones she was brought into the consciousness of her "Divine Sonship." She began to understand the necessity of accepting God as First Cause, and she understood that the great I Am Presence was within her. Through diligent prayer and through great consciousness, her leg began to grow, and by the time she had reached the age of thirty, the leg had grown to match the right one perfectly. Today, there is no way that one could detect that her two legs had not always been perfect. Interestingly, too, her leg grew just so far: It did not grow out ten feet, just the amount needed to come into completion with her perfect self.

Can this seeming miracle be explained? Not in man-idea terms—but, as expressions of God, we know that nothing is impossible. To paraphrase the famous statement of St. Augustine, "Miracles are not contrary to nature, only contrary to what we hold in consciousness concerning God." We should expect miracles daily in our lives, because they will and must occur when we come into the realization of the One Presence and One Power. Healing in body, mind, and spirit will have to occur, *no matter what the outer condition*, when God is completely accepted. God is limitless in His perfection, so there is nothing that God cannot create and nothing that God cannot overcome. As expressions of God, it is our inheritance to have this same power—but we must claim it. When we do, we come into the healing image.

OUR FAITH

IN THE EPISTLE of James it is stated that the prayer of faith shall save him that is sick (James 5:15). When we understand that effective prayer is *never* made until faith is established, we can see how prayer *in faith* must be the healing process. Faith is always based on an understanding—an acceptance—whether of "things" of this world or the deeper awareness of "things" spiritual (energized). In establishing the healing image, the first step must be an examination of what to establish as a frame of reference, the authority relied upon as the espression of Truth. Whatever we believe to be the First Cause (intelligence) will be that which gives us faith.

If we place our faith on the material things, ideas, and concepts of the world, we cannot possibly come into the complete healing image. Everything in the physical world, whether ideas or things, is ever changing and never constant. Centuries ago, Ovid stated that all is ebb and flow, ever changing, never constant, and everything that is born of this world bears within its womb the seeds of change. If we place our faith on that which is ever changing and never constant, how can we possibly develop a healing image? It cannot be done, because the outer is ever changing, so there is no substance in what we rely on out there. Substance is quite different from that which is material. Material things are ever changing and are never the same from one second to the next. Substance, however, is ever constant, always absolute, and always reliable. Hence, the basis of what really is in Truth is substance, and substance, of course, is that which emanates from one source and has only perfect manifestation as its objective.

ONE SUBSTANTIAL POWER

THERE IS ONLY one substantial Power and Presence on this earth, and that is God. If we place our attention and give our authority to the substantial One Presence and One Power in our lives, then *all* of our images will emanate from God and nothing becomes impossible. This is the only complete faith, and it is the only faith which allows the images of perfect health, prosperity, wisdom, joy, and happiness to come into our lives. The recognition of the I Am Presence, God Within, builds whatever we need into our daily activities without any exception. This principle is clearly enunciated by Jesus in many ways, but particularly when he tells us first to seek the kingdom of heaven and all else shall be brought unto us, as well as in the great Commandment: Love God.

It is interesting how the men of great consciousness who founded the government of the United States *always* stressed where we should place our authority. How they knew and understood the law! Time after time, they emphasized that this nation was to be established *under God* and that *In God we trust.* Obviously, if we are under God, God is our authority—and if it is in God we trust, then again, God is our authority. When the authority is placed at the highest, then all under that authority must express in perfection, and all that manifests through mind will be perfect. The healing image will naturally emerge full grown and full flowering.

THE CONSCIOUSNESS OF
GOD'S POTENTIAL

IN THE BUDDHIST faith much is made of the lotus. Many who have visited in Southeast Asia have seen the lotus growing without human cultivation. The lotus can emerge from the very darkest and most dismal swamps. In fact, it is in the darkened waters that the lotus "springs forth." However, the lotus does not manifest its beauty and its perfection until it begins to unfold. The "Eightfold Path" of Buddhism uses the eight layers of the lotus as the symbol of this expression. The lotus does not begin to express its innate beauty until it begins to unfold, and its complete beauty is never fully expressed until all eight layers of petals are open. The symbology here is rather obvious: We cannot come into the God Perfection within until fully opened to the consciousness of God's potential.

The story of the Phoenix rising from the ashes is another "myth" that is full of truth—the truth that in knowledge of God, all is possible. The Phoenix (a great bird) rose from the ashes of fire (a purifying process) because in the fire a new dimension, the true dimension, was discovered. This discovery brought the consciousness of how to overcome all and how to come into perfection. The lotus, the Phoenix, and many other real and mythological manifestations are simply illustrations of the "overcoming" that takes place when the consciousness is purged of all ideas which are not God-oriented. It is the realization of our unique expression of God (created in the image and likeness of God) which builds the healing image, the prosperity image, the happiness image, and, in fact, all images which are helpful, uplifting, and healing.

It is the lack of the consciousness of God as First Cause (Essence or I Am Presence) that gives us the images that create fear: the images of sickness, isolation, failure, unhappiness, and depression. Ralph Waldo Emerson said that we should never underestimate man's propensity for degradation or exaltation. Whether our experiences will be degrading ones or exalting ones will depend upon the authority(-ies) we have in our lives.

If we are feeling ill, unhappy, depressed, or lonely, we should ask ourselves: What am I making First Principle in my life? Have I accepted that I am created in the image and likeness of God? Have I loved God above and beyond all else? Any type of limitation in our acceptance of God as our Father, as our protector, or as our savior will bring negative conditions in either our body, mind, affairs, or in them all.

SEE GOD IN ALL THINGS

THERE ARE MANY ways in which we can come into a consciousness of God Within (the I Am Presence). We see God when we see life. We see God when we know Truth. We are aware of God when we love. When true knowledge comes, we know that God is intelligence: when we accept the Spirit in ourselves, we get some understanding of God, and when we feel deeply about some good, we know that the soul is an expression of God's perfection. When we know that the Sun will shine and that the law of gravity is always working, we become aware of God as Principle. Each of these manifestations is an aspect of God: life, truth, love, intelligence, soul, spirit, and principle. When we fail to look for God behind any of these great aspects, we have yet to know God. Often, we hear individuals referring to God as Soul (or Soul as God). This is in error, because as important as it is, soul is just one aspect of God. They are on the right track, but they have a limited consciousness of the nature of God. When we begin to understand the many potentials of God and manifestations of God in evidence around us, we take a giant step toward the realization of the healing image—the perfect image of God which each and every individual is. What we manifest in our lives is up to us and is determined through our consciousness, but our very being is an expression of God. We can accept our inheritance or we can deny it, but, no matter what we do, we are in the image and likeness of God.

TURN TO THE TRUTH

WE HAVE SO many ways in which we can deny God and lose contact with the wonderful healing that can be ours simply for its acceptance. Often we feel ill, or we feel that there is something before us that we cannot overcome. What should we do first when these feelings come upon us? Should we rush to the medicine chest, the doctor, or the "expert"? No! What we should do is turn to what we know is Truth (the I Am expression of God) and refuse to accept the condition at its face value. We must realize that the condition is a reflection of mind and raise our thought. Jesus demonstrated this when he said, "Get thee behind me, Satan." He refused to entertain such thoughts in his mind. Instead, he affirmed his Divine Sonship, and he sought to grasp more deeply the concept that "the Father and I are one." This was the perfect healing expression and image to hold, and it is one that we must all learn to use.

THE PSALMS PROVIDE UNDERSTANDING

ONE OF THE greatest of all understandings of the healing image is to be found in the great Twenty-seventh Psalm. In this magnificent affirmation of where our strength lies and of what should be and really is our authority, the Psalmist writes, "The Lord is my might and my salvation; whom shall I fear? The Lord is the strength of my life; of whom shall I be afraid?" Indeed, with God as our might (power), with God as our salvation, and with God as our strength, what possible fear can we have? What can possibly harm us in our God-perfection? Even though we may be experiencing great adversity at this time, we must know that God is our salvation. The understanding of *salvation* brings great assistance to the lifting of consciousness. The word is derived from *salvage*, which means to bring back into usable form, to resurrect. The preferred dictionary meaning of salvation is *freedom from clinging to the phenomenal world of appearance and reunion with ultimate reality*. With God as the cornerstone of our understanding (our authority base and frame of reference), the God in us is resurrected and brought back into our consciousness. The healing must then take place.

Emmet Fox, in speaking of the 27th Psalm and the passage just cited, makes this observation: "[This phrase of the psalm] postulates not merely the existence of God, but the living Presence of God in man, for the Lord here means your own Indwelling Christ, the I Am. Then it goes on to state that God in you, the Inner Light, is no mere passive or static presence, but a dynamic power to do everything for you that you can possibly need to have done. Just consider what this one phrase promises —light, salvation and strength."

How beautifully the psalmist wrote of the protecting, healing, and "enlightening" Power that dwells within, just waiting to be released by the individual! We should read the 23rd and 91st psalms and find the same understanding. For example, in the 91st Psalm the author writes, "He who dwells in the secret place of the most High shall abide under the shadow of the Almighty." And Moses wrote for the 90th Psalm, "Lord, thou hast been our dwelling place in all generations." These beautiful and mighty expressions become meaningful to us only when we recognize that God is not some nebulous figure floating in the sky but is an indwelling spirit, a complete expression within us waiting to be born through our consciousness. We must learn that we are spiritual beings and that we worship in spirit and Truth.

To worship is to accept whatever we have decided is important without reservation. When we worship in true spirit and complete Truth, we are worshiping God and, therefore, have created in our minds the proper understanding of God; we now have the perfect image. Naturally, the perfect image we are now worshiping is God as expressed through all of His aspects: life, truth, love, soul, intelligence, spirit, and principle. The image is now complete, and within that perfect understanding of God there is the perfect healing image, the perfect happiness image, and the perfect prosperity image—the perfect all-in-all, the Alpha and the Omega.

THE PERFECT IMAGE

IF WE GRASP and hold on to the mighty words of Jesus, there is no way in which we can avoid coming into the full realization of God within (the I Am Presence). We now have the perfect image for perfect life-expression and not just for healing: "Our Father, which art in heaven, hallowed be thy name; thy kingdom come, thy will be done, on Earth as it is in Heaven." Accept these words with deep understanding. The perfect image now lives in our hearts and will have to express in mind and body.

The Perfect Revolution

OVID, THE GREAT PHILOSOPHER of long ago, stated that all is ebb and flow, ever changing, and never constant. This is a very basic understanding of all the "things" of the world and all that has come into materialization. It is true, too, of our thought processes. Everything and every thought is changing and revolving in various ways and is never constant. As a result of the constant changing, we become confused and do not understand what these "forces" seem to be that disturb us so. Unless there is a solid foundation for anything (great understanding lying behind the surface), there is bound to be great insecurity. It is like living on the shifting sands and feeling a constant undercurrent that is unsettling to both the mind and the body. Only when Principle comes into life and into understanding does the revolving cease and the evolving start.

GOING BACK TO BASIC PRINCIPLE

THE WORD *revolution* comes from *revolve*, meaning going back to something that has already been manifested or understood. The only meaningful revolution is when we go back to basic Principle (Source, Cause, God, the I Am Presence). We can keep revolving and revolting until all of life and experience become a nightmare. Can you imagine constantly going through a revolving door, just going around and around with no destination and no feeling of accomplishment, never a terminal and never a goal? Those who keep "revolving" in their consciousness concerning what they are and of what they are a part are always "revolting," striking out at what is around them and forever in a revolving circuit of disillusion, disappointment, and depression. They are constantly in a turmoil and in a state of constant antagonism against themselves and all around them. They are often even unkindly, but not incorrectly, called *revolting*. Just like Don Quixote, many of us live in a constant state of revolution, always striking out but not knowing at what.

If we begin to revolve back to the consciousness of Source (God) we come home again, and there comes into our life and understanding a great consciousness of peace, harmony, joy, and creativity. Without reverting back, revolving, to an awareness of what one is and of what one is a part, there will be a constant revolution going on in the mind, which will create a disturbance of body, mind, and spirit.

The only effective and lasting revolution is one that brings us into an awareness of what we are. From this consciousness (awareness) all the aspects of God within us will develop, and the revolution will become an evolution of the soul back into its original awareness of the great Presence within.

AWARENESS OF GOD

EACH OF US has a revolution daily, and every thought we bring into our consciousness is sowing the seed of revolution. Whether the seed will evolve into a happier, more joyous, and healthy state, or produce strife, unhappiness, and illness will depend upon whether the seed has been sown in the fertile soil of God Consciousness or in a consciousness of only the physical manifestations upon the Earth. We choose between the kingdom and the shadows by virtue of what we accept as the Truth. Our minds are ever shifting and never constant; hence, we feel great "un-ease" in our lives until we have established a firm foundation in counsciousness.

We revolve into a consciousness which gives great structure and great strength when we make a firm foundation of the awareness of God and become Godseekers. As Jesus told us, "Seek ye first the kingdom of heaven and all else shall be brought unto you." The nature of matter is to change; there is no constancy. There cannot be. We can organize, change, and direct change. We can also become "drifters" and be in constant turmoil, not knowing from day to day or from hour to hour where our strength lies. The great revolution, the only meaningful revolution, occurs for us when we shift our attention from the manifestations of the world and place it where there is constancy and permanence, on the I Am Presence, the awareness of God.

THE AMERICAN REVOLUTION

THE AMERICAN REVOLUTION was perhaps the greatest revolution in the history of the world because the Founders were so aware of the absolute inportance of establishing as a frame of reference for the new nation an awareness of the one solid, substantial Power in the world: God. It is not accidental that the basic language of the Declaration of Independence and the coinage of the United States clearly stated that this nation was to be established in and under God. This was the great revolution that occurred in the world in 1776. It was an affirmation that the basic structure and development of the nation would be "under God." God would be at the underpinning (the understanding) of the acts and actions of the nation, and thereby of the citizens of the nation. This was the basic awareness of the Founders, and they never departed for a moment from this understanding.

There are many lessons in the American Revolution that can be applied to our own lives. In fact, the concepts of the architects of the American Revolution, if adopted by each individual in his or her own life, would liberate, and bring great harmony and joy. The only failure of the American Revolution occurred after the Revolution: the precepts were not followed by many who came later and who did not have the basic understanding or the great consciousness of the very wise persons who led this nation into its birth. In some respects much of what has come since the Revolution reminds me of George Bernard Shaw's famous statement, "The only trouble with Christianity is that it has never been tried."

THE GOD POTENTIAL WITHIN US

WHAT WAS THE cardinal concept of the architects of the United States? If we read the words of the Declaration of Independence, the Constitution, and the Federalist Papers closely, we are immediately struck by the belief in the equality, in essence, of every individual—and the belief that when the uniqueness is understood as stemming from God, only great harmony, peace, growth, and creativity can emerge. "All men are created equal," "in God we trust," and "under God" are just a few of the many statements illustrating the understanding that each individual is an expression of God and has the potential of a son or daughter of God. There was no "big brother" concept, but there was the understanding that when a number work together in harmony (a God-like attribute), only good can emerge.

The dominant theme of the writers of the words we should now be governed by was the God potential within each and every human being. This threw over the political philosophy which had stood for more than 1,600 years in Europe: the philosophy of the "divine right" of kings, the concept that we can only become that which our physical fathers were, and the belief that people were superior or inferior according to their birth. This philosophy should have been destroyed by the American Revolution, which was a revolution of consciousness more than anything else. It was revolving of consciousness back to Cause, Essence, God. It was a revolution designed to destroy forever the myth of special privilege due to physical birth; instead, it required the placing of emphasis on each individual's ability and willingness to activate God-given talents and potentials.

FREEDOM REQUIRES TREMENDOUS RESPONSIBILITY

IT WAS A revolution that required the acceptance of great responsibility on the part of every person. No longer could the blame for failure, sickness, limitation, or for good be placed on the shoulders of the feudal lord or a priest of a church. The American Revolution was designed to give and provide a framework for the development of personal liberty and personal growth. The American "dream" required, though, that the individual bear his or her own "cross" and not lay it down before some feudal lord (called government) or before some priest; one was to be responsible for his or her own consciousness.

What a magnificent design, and what a wonderful affirmation of faith in God-in-us was expressed by the Founders of the United States! It is almost beyond belief in light of the present state of consciousness, collectively, in the country. Truly, the Founders attempted to revolve humankind back into its native God-awareness. However, even like our Father in Heaven, they recognized that each person had to shoulder his or her responsibility and had to pull his or her own weight. They knew that freedom required a tremendous sense of responsibility. When responsibility is evaded, freedom is eroded. When we accept our God-potential and our divine inheritance, we must also accept the responsibility this potential and inheritance places upon us. We cannot have one without the other.

Each of us can begin to see in his or her own life the great plan of the American Revolutionary Founders whenever we accept, in our consciousness, our relationship with the I Am Presence (the Christ, Cosmic Within). This acceptance brings a great feeling of freedom, joy, harmony, and creativity, but it also brings a sense of responsibility and a great need to establish guidelines for living in this free and wonderful environment. This is also true with respect to the Constitution of the United States. Where are the "laws" to be found in this great guide for effective government and living? They are not there. The Constitution of the United States was a great *guide* for living in a society of free people, and to live within the Constitution required great responsibility.

As we Americans have refused to accept our responsibility and have placed more and more emphasis on "letting government do it" for us, we have been losing freedom. Giving up responsibility always means giving up freedom as well; hence, we must have guidelines for effective living in our own lives in order to live freely and abundantly. Jesus put it so perfectly when he said, "If the son therefore shall make you free, ye shall be free indeed" (John 8:36). How wonderfully he was telling us that through our acceptance of our Sonship, through our awareness of what we are and of what we are a part, and through the acceptance of the responsibility that divine Sonship requires, we become free—free indeed!

THE POTENTIAL RICHNESS OF LIFE

JESUS NEVER LAID down specific man-made laws by which we must live. He laid down guidelines which we could choose to follow or not; it was up to us. He told us of the great benefits that would come to us through the acceptance of the responsibility that living up to our potential required; but he clearly stated that these guidelines were Cosmic (God) Laws and on the Earth we could choose to follow or not to follow them. He added that if we followed these guidelines we would find the potential richness of life most fulfilling and fulfilled; if we chose not to do so, we would find limitation, chaos, unhappiness, and disharmony. He gave us the Great Commandment and the Second one like unto it: Love. He told us clearly that these were the guidelines to perfect living and perfect expression in all aspects of life and not laws that had to be followed.

We have free will to accept or reject any guideline, but we should expect to become an "outlaw" to all that is good in the guidance if we choose to ignore it. He gave us the Principle for the perfect expression of life, but placed upon us the responsibility of acceptance of the guidance. The authors of our Constitution had such faith in the wisdom of people "under God" that they provided, through the Constitution, the perfect pattern for living in a social system. They realized, however, that not all of us would accept the responsibility of guidance, so a Supreme

Court was established to determine whether or not future law-makers would understand and work within the framework of the guidelines.

Our Creator also provided us with a framework within which we could live, and live abundantly—a perfect body and a perfect mind (both perfect in potential). Through understanding the laws of God (the guidance He has given) we can find the perfect manner in which to express our individualized aspect of Godhood. Through ignoring or not accepting the responsibility of living within the guidance, we lose the freedom of choice and the freedom of perfect living. It is my belief that many who established the Declaration of Independence and the Constitution were patterning both after the great design of the Master Creator, God. Certainly, they recognized God as Source, Cause, and Essence. They also recognized us as sons and daughters of God with the God potential within. Through this recognition they provided a perfect framework for living in society in harmony, justice, freedom, and happiness.

Our lack of willingness to accept the principle upon which these great people established this framework for abundance is the only thing that can destroy the United States. No external force or military power can harm or destroy us. Nothing can hurt us in any way if we stick to principle—and this principle of perfect living in society was established beautifully for us. Of course, there are and were flaws, because with all of their insight and all of their understanding, the Founders were mortals; they had not come completely into the I Am Consciousness. Even with the flaws, however, no more perfect manner of establishing a government providing for harmony and abundance has ever been enunciated than that brought forth by the Founders of this nation more than two hundred years ago.

THE PERSONAL REVOLUTION

DOES THE American Revolution have some definite application to us other than the fact that we are American citizens and, therefore, subject to the Constitution of the United States? I think it does, and it can profoundly assist each of us in establishing our own revolution. A revolution in the outer, which is often bloody and destructive in its manifestations, can often be most peaceful, harmonious, and uplifting on the inner plane of consciousness. Our own personal revolution, to be effective, must be evolving back to First Cause and establishing God as First Cause, Essence, and Cosmic. Just as the American Revolution recognized that all was "under God" and all were equal in the "sight of God," so must we claim the divine inheritance for ourselves and all others. We must take our attention away from lack, illness, and unhappiness and resolve it back to an awareness of the I Am Presence (the Christ within). We must claim our divine Sonship, which is our right and the truth of us. We must make God the First Cause in our lives.

Whatever we observe and whatever we bring into our consciousness, we must purify with the awareness of the Presence of God. We must always demand our inheritance as the child of God and must claim it for all humans. This is the practice of Love. If you were left one hundred thousand dollars in a valid and honestly drawn will and someone came in and took over that sum, would you not demand that justice be done? Would you not go to the courts and claim your rights? Would you not sue that your rights be recognized? Of course you would. We have a responsibility to see that justice triumphs, but how many even recognize that they have every right to all of the abundance of the world that they need? There are very few, indeed. Therefore, the first principle we must establish in revolving into the high consciousness that we have as an inheritance is the recognition of God as our Parent and God as our unlimited source.

RECOGNIZE THE SOURCE

TO FURTHER THE perfect revolution in ourselves and to develop the highest possible consciousness, we must recognize the guidelines for perfect living and perfect expression that have been provided for us. These are everywhere, but we must not simply note them and pass them by. What are the basic guidelines that our Parent (Cause) has provided for us? Do they have to be pointed out to us? In many respects, I believe that if they have to be identified for us, we are not ready for the perfect revolution back to our Parent (the I Am Presence). We see these guidelines, however, by observing the life around us. What is life? What causes life? How does life evolve? If we are involved with these questions, we are observing a God-given guideline: Life is an expression and an aspect of God. When we recognize the value of life and the source of life, our living will change. The revolution is under way because we are now on the road to comprehending God, and the basic guideline (loving God) begins to be both comprehended and adhered to. "My Father and I are one" and "Be ye perfect even as your Father in heaven" were statements made by Jesus to help us understand the guideposts and read the signs along the highway of life.

THE PERFECT ORDERLINESS
OF THE UNIVERSE

ANOTHER WONDERFUL GUIDELINE we have been given is the perfection and orderliness of the universe. Dr. Saltzman, a famed biochemist and vice chancellor of the University of California at San Diego, has stated that there are three concepts that every scientist must accept and hold to: (1) there is perfect order in the universe; (2) we can comprehend that order; and (3) it is good to comprehend that order. What a magnificent understanding of the potential within us and the limitless perfection within which we move! Only we can disturb perfection, and we cause disruption when we fail to understand what we are and of what we are a part. All scientific discoveries have come about because we have faith that there is greater "there" than our senses can now detect. A sense of the mystical is the true sower of all scientific inquiry, but that sense of the mystic, and that drive to discover, is never present until we understand to some degree that there is perfect order in the universe and we can comprehend that order. The greater the awareness of the orderliness and the perfection in the universe, the greater the discoveries will always be. Even the word *discover* tells us much: to uncover, take off the "wraps" of that which has always been there but hidden by the blindness of the senses.

In understanding the perfect orderliness of the universe, we truly come closer to God and to an awareness of the I Am Presence, *present* everywhere. As Paul said, "God is in all, with all, through all," which is a beautiful affirmation of the Presence of God. Through the recognition of this guideline one begins to understand that God is Principle. *When we know that there is one basic principle guiding all*, and if the guidance is followed, there can only be perfect manifestation! How freeing that is! How joyous we must become when we know and are deeply aware of the perfect Principle active in all life, all affairs, all problems, and all manifestations. Our revolution will be successful for us, not just now, but forever when our consciousness accepts the perfect principle of God. When this happens we become free, and we are indeed free!

A NEW FORCE

REVOLUTIONS IN NATIONS begin when there is a consciousness that something is missing in life, that there is more to gain by throwing off the old concepts and old ways and adopting a new concept and a new way. Most revolutions in the world (at least, in the political world) stem from avarice, greed, envy, jealousy, etc. (various aspects of "deadly sins"). Most revolutions of a political nature fail to improve the lot of the people and simply substitute one form of tyranny for another. One set of rules is instigated in place of an old set, with the result that nothing really changes except the leadership of the tyranny. Only a few political revolutions have ever benefited the lot of humanity or improved its physical condition. The American Revolution was one such, and it gave birth to the French Revolution a few years later, which was built on the same principles as the American: equality and fraternity.

The American Revolution improved the lot of humankind and set forth a new force in the world, or, at least, a force that had been dormant for several thousand years, because it was not a revolution based on greed, avarice, jealousy, or hatred. It was based, in the minds of the revolutionary leaders, on faith in humanity, the awareness of the God-potential of each individual, loving appreciation of the right of all to various opinions (God provided us with free will), and, most importantly, the complete acceptance of the unlimited power for good to triumph when an awareness of God was the foundation of all action. There was no equivocation on the part of our Founders in their complete acceptance that humanity was an expression of God, and, as God's expression, the nature of God is in humankind. This is what made the American Revolution a new force in the world. It freed the bottled-up energy for good which had been stifled for thousands of years by the denial that all was "under God" and all were "inheritors of God."

In George III, the belief in God playing favorites was epitomized (divine right of kings), and our Founders found that the king, in a sense, had become an idol—he represented God. This was not the truth, and they became free, and we become free, when it is discovered and held that the real truth is: All humans are expressions of God and inheritors, in potential, of that which is their Parent's. Our revolution was successful, not just for a few years or months, but for several hundred years. It can be reactivated in all of its drive, thrust, and beauty whenever we again claim our inheritance as expressions of God. There will be no envy, greed, lust, or avarice in our hearts if we know that there is an abundance of everything when our trust is placed in God.

A CHANGE IN CONSCIOUSNESS

IN ORDER FOR one's own revolution to make an effective difference in one's life and to bring fulfillment, happiness, joy, peace, health, and harmony, a change in consciousness will be required. It will require, just as it required in the American Revolution, an awareness that something is missing in one's life. Do we lack harmony, peace, joy, health, or enthusiasm? Then should we not start revolting against that which we feel is limiting, that which is unhealthy, or that which is inharmonious? If we use our minds at all, we shall realize that the things that bring distress and limitation to us are not the outer things of the world—not money, not illness per se, not lack of education, and not our environment—but, rather, our ideas concerning the things of the world. Where have we placed our emphasis? Has it been on the *manifestation*, which is, of course, what the environment is? The environment is never cause; it is always effect. We begin our effective revolution when we realize that the *condition* does not need changing—only the *consciousness*. When we come to this understanding we are creating a really effective, meaningful, lasting, and helpful evolution. We are working with first principle, and, as with the founders of the American Revolution, we are identified with that which is eternal, uplifting, and freeing.

TRUST IN GOD

ONE SHOULD ASK oneself: "Who or what is controlling in my life?" If the answer is anything but an awareness of God, we must revolt against that consciousness. Just as George III was the symbol of all authority and God's selectivity, we must realize that wherever we place our faith, we are accepting that symbol as our control (our God). We must become God-seekers ("Seek ye first the kingdom of heaven and all else shall be brought unto you"), and then we shall be able to make the evolution from the consciousness of limitation to one of abundance. We must revolt against any person, idea, or thing in which we place our complete trust. We must learn to think consciously as this nation's Founders did: "In God I trust." In trusting God we find that we really "come home again"; and we are freed of all binding restriction that must come when we make idols of the people, things, or ideas of the world. Placing God in first place as first Principle and Cause will always make the revolutionary change in thought perfect and complete.

It is so freeing and enlightening to realize that the words of Paul (2 Cor. 4:4), "Their unbelieving minds are so blinded by the god of this passing age, that the gospel of the glory of Christ, who is the very image of God, cannot dawn upon them and bring them light," are true. We can always lift the blindness to great enlightenment through changing our concept of God. The most effective of all revolutions of men or nations occurs when a solid appreciation and love for God takes place. This establishment of an effective understanding of God is found through observing the works of God ("By their fruits you shall know them"). When our consciousness evolves into understanding life, truth, love, principle, soul, and spirit, we are placing God and Cause as first in our lives. We have come to the point where we accept our own indivisibility under God just as the founders of this nation did. We must take off the blinders of this age: the senses.

We must put on the armament of God, which is seeking of Source, and our revolution will bring peace, harmony, joy, and freedom into our lives.

THE VICTORIOUS REVOLUTION

In 1 John 5:4–5, we are told that "every child of God is victor of the godless world. The victory that defeats the world is our faith, for who is victor over the world but he who believes?" Yes, the victorious revolution, the meaningful revolution, and the lasting revolution for an individual or a nation is one which brings the individual into a consciousness of the I Am Presence, into an awareness of First Cause, the Essence, Principle, the Cosmic, and the Christ. The victory is always to those who know their identity, who believe in the goal they seek, and who are aware of the good that is set before them.

The beauty of the American Revolution was that it was based solely on the "God in man" knowledge, and as we attempt to improve our lot in the world and for eternity, this, too, must be what we hold onto. Our own revolution is complete, successful, and everlasting when our consciousness rests completely in our I Am Presence.

Let us remember, as the great psalmist wrote, "He that dwelleth in the secret place of the most High shall abide under the shadow of the Almighty" (Ps. 91:1).

Make Your Labor Fulfilling

ECCLESIASTES 3:22: ". . . there is nothing better than that a man should rejoice in his own works; for that is his portion: for who shall bring him to see what shall be after him?"

The poet Robert Frost once wrote: "The world is full of willing people . . . some willing to work, the rest willing to let them."

Kahlil Gibran wrote in *The Prophet* some very effective concepts regarding labor:

> You work that you may keep peace with the earth and
>   the soul of the earth.
> For to be idle is to become a stranger unto the seasons,
>   and to step out of life's procession, that marches in
>   majesty and proud submission toward the infinite.
> When you work you are a flute through whose heart the
>   whispering of the hours turns to music.
> Which of you would be a reed, dumb and silent, when
>   all else sings together in unison?

Always you have been told that work is a curse and
labour a misfortune.

But I say to you that when you work you fulfil a part of
earth's furthest dream, assigned to you when that
dream was born.

And in keeping yourself with labour you are in truth loving life.

Work is love made visible.

Gibran also said, "To love life through labor is to be intimate
with life's inmost secret."

WORK WILL FULFILL
ACCORDING TO BELIEF

WHAT SCRIPTURE, Frost, Gibran and other great
teachers really have been saying is simply this: "How do *you*
think of your job, your work?" Is it a means to an end or is it
viewed as a new expression, an opportunity to open new dimensions in life? We can control our viewpoint! The very term *point
of view* means that we have established a *frame of reference*—a
position from which we are now "viewing," "visioning," all
aspects of our life. This includes the concept of our labor, our
work. Don't forget where the word *provision* comes from: *pro*
("ahead"), *visio* ("vision," "viewpoint"). The word *provide*
comes from the same base. Our work will fulfill us according
to our own belief—our attitude.

Confucius once said (truly, and not in a fortune cookie):
"Choose a job you love and you will never have to work a day
in your life."

How do we choose a job? We can readily see this done when
we select a certain profession and train for that profession, such
as medical doctor, dentist, nurse, lawyer, professor-teacher, or

any of the professions. But are we not all involved in a "profession"? Are we not all truly working at what we have professed (*pro*-"before"; *fateri*-"confess," "believe in")? What we believe in *is* what our job will become: It is what we have "professed"—put into our world.

LIFE IS TO BE ENJOYED

IF LABOR IS not fulfilling, it is because we don't believe it to be. Lack of motivation always makes for drudgery. It always will. We must realize that we are craftspersons molding and shaping a part of God's creation. God intended that life be enjoyed (not the Calvin-Wesleyan idea of suffering).

How is motivation changed so that we can love the job? It is changed by finding a new dimension of self which can be quickened and brought alive through the work experience, and then by doing it!

It has been said, "The best way to keep good intentions from dying is to execute them" and "Seek and ye will find, knock and the door will be opened to you." But be aware that we are always seeking through our vision of our world and of ourselves. This is the key to making anything fulfilling in life: Know what you are and set your vision on a higher dimension in whatever you are currently doing. See new vistas, new peaks, and go to the mountaintop where you will have the fulfillment. Remember, Jesus did not put down fishing when he picked his first disciples, Peter and Andrew. He gave them a new and higher vision of the possibilities in their work ("Come with me and be fishers of men").

If you are out of work, retired, incapacitated in some way, or have a job which seems very routine and nonstimulating, ask yourself, "Have I truly looked first to acknowledge what I am and secondarily to the work experience? Or have I expected some kind of work experience to provide me with fulfillment? Am I saying, 'I will be so happy if I get this job'?'' If you are, the job will not fulfill the promise in your life. It cannot. You have put the cart before the horse. First, determine—know—who you are, and then the job will come into existence or the present position will change because *you* have changed.

WE ARE RESPONSIBLE FOR OUR OWN FULFILLMENT

WE ARE RESPONSIBLE for the fulfillment or lack of fulfillment in our work—not the boss, not the company, not the financing company, not our co-workers, not our environment. None of these is responsible for our fulfillment.

Remember, our responsibility is to respond to our real self. An individual is an undivided expression of the Infinite. Remember, too, that *response* is the basis of the word *responsibility*. We find and accept the right responsibility when we have correctly responded to our true nature.

FINDING THE RIGHT OCCUPATION

MOST OF US are highly preoccupied with what we are *not*; we don't, then, have the opportunity to find the right occupation. Think of the word *pre-occupation*—not involved with Truth—involved, instead, with all of the vicissitudes, limitations, and difficulties the world believes in. Become occupied with the true nature of self and God and set aside preoccupation with ideas of limitation; the proper occupation will then come into form (fulfillment).

If your present state of work—or lack of work—is difficult for you right now, ask yourself, ''Am I *pre*-occupied with this lack; with the belief that I cannot achieve what I desire; with the concept of limitation in my education, experience, and environment?" How can we find our occupation when we are *pre*-occupied (already occupied in mind)? Become involved (in tune) with your true nature—make *that* your primary occupation—and the manifestation (fulfillment) will come no matter what the world may believe about this. Many theologians believe that the Original Sin was our *pre*-occupation with form, conditions, the physical. Baptism was devised to "wash away" the idea of form being the all-in-all. Baptism, in a way, is a rehearsal for a greater performance on the true stage of life. All of us seem to be living our lives in rehearsals—waiting for something to happen, waiting for the right "opportunity," preparing for a certain degree or certificate. A rehearsal is always preparation but never the final production. Many of us go through life in a constant state of "rehearsal"; there can then be no fulfillment.

LIVE IN THE NOW

WE HEAR THIS so often on the job: "If I just get through this, then . . ."; "When I get the promotion, I will . . ."; "Thank God, it's Friday"; "My vacation is just so many days away. . . ." In all of these things we are *rehearsing* and never truly *performing* at a level that will allow for complete fulfillment. Fulfillment doesn't come through *rehearsal*; it comes through *doing* (actually performing). Most of us are *pre*-occupied with preparation, rehearsal, so the great occupational possibilities escape us. We don't live in the now; we live in the land of "what-if," which is nonproductive (nonperforming).

Look for the good in the now and joy will be in your heart. As it is stated in Ecclesiastes 3:22: "There is nothing better than that a man should rejoice in his own works; for that is his portion: for who shall bring him to see what shall be after him?"

Affirm: "I am one with the Infinite, and therefore through the proper work, through the proper channels, I will express my unique individualism within the Infinite." This takes us out of rehearsal into the fulfillment of the promise which is within each and every individual. We are no longer *pre*-occupied, so we can now turn our full attention to the right occupation. We can find fulfillment in whatever we are doing (or want to do).

THE RIGHT LABOR IS THERE FOR US

WE MUST UNDERSTAND that we are an expression of the Infinite and therefore have access to all, which includes labor that is joyous, fulfilling, and complete. As John W. Doorly once put it, "Humanity will never be perfect until it recognizes that because the Infinite is infinite there can only be one. You can't have anything outside of infinity. . . . There is nothing outside of that Infinite *One*, and 'in Him we live, and move, and have our being.' " Naturally, in that One, the right labor is there for us, but we must open our eyes to the Truth and not be *pre*-occupied with negative concepts that are available if searched for in any occupation, any type of labor.

If the "work" we do in our life feels burdensome, overwhelming, and stressful, why not stop analyzing the work and start analyzing our own consciousness? What do we really believe concerning "the Infinite is infinite—there can only be one"? In a very real manner, this is following Jesus' admonition of "Seek ye first the kingdom of heaven and all else shall be brought unto you." In the concept of oneness—with all possibilities—there is the right occupation for the complete fulfillment of each individual; however, the right occupation cannot be found while we are *pre*-occupied (our mind is already employed) with concepts of negativity. Get back to the understanding of *the Infinite is infinite*. Become a seeker after this Great

Presence and the beliefs concerning the occupation must, by law, change.

Everything starts in belief and ends in form. Thought— Action—Manifestation, the Law of Expression, is the law of the universe. If our thoughts are *pre*-occupied with all sorts of limitations, there is no room for the occupation (job) that fulfills. There is "no room in the inn." Jesus is quoted as saying (John 6:27), "Labor not for the meat which perisheth, but for that meat which endureth unto everlasting life, which the Son of man shall give unto you: for him hath God the Father sealed." This is a powerful statement reaffirming the necessity not to spend our time laboring to earn a living but to live while earning. If we spend our time laboring for that which is temporary— as all worldly things are—we never have the experience of joy, harmony, health, and peace in our lives. It is through adopting an attitude of seeing a new dimension of good in every activity that we find peace, joy, and wholeness. This, too, is loving God —seeing the Presence behind every activity.

EVERYTHING BEGINS
WITH THOUGHT

JESUS STATED, "I come to minister, not to be ministered unto." Many of us "labor under" conditions, circumstances and activities of our world. We feel manipulated, controlled, and directed by people and circumstances around us. We are laboring under afflictions which we have accepted in our world. We are not here to be ministered to by these outer conditions and circumstances; we are here to express the truth—the truth of the I Am Presence (the Truth of the God expression which I Am)— but because we feel belabored by our work and our surroundings, we have lost that freedom to minister and have become the "administered." It is through understanding that labor is the activity resulting from mind-idea that we are set free.

When we recognize this fact—that everything first begins in thought (mind) and then passes through activity to bring forth the manifestation—we are in the consciousness that labor (activity) is the necessary link between thought and manifestation. Hence, if we feel put upon in our endeavors (labor) then we must change the thought. Thought always comes first, not the labor. Labor is simply the agency through which thought must pass. When this becomes central in our thinking, we will realize the importance of looking for the good in what we are doing, and if we cannot seemingly find the good, we must learn to go back through the process to thought, where it all began. When we change our thinking, we change our labor. We are no longer ministered to—we are now the minister.

Gibran put it very well when he wrote, "Work is love made visible." If we would realize that labor is the catalyst between thought and manifestation (form), we would spend no time berating and bewailing our work; rather, we would start analyzing our thoughts, realizing that they are what is making the task seem onerous. We become the "minister" of our own labors only when we recognize that our thought world controls; otherwise our thoughts scatter, seeking a goal in the negative around us, and we then feel, and really are, under the administration of another. (In Jesus' words: "I come to minister, not to be ministered unto.")

Ralph Waldo Emerson wrote:

Each man has his own vocation. The talent is the call. There is one direction in which all space is open to him. He has faculties silently inviting him thither to endless exertion. He is like a ship in a river; he runs against obstruction on every side but one, on that one side all obstruction is taken away and he sweeps serenely over a deepening channel into an infinite sea. This talent and this call depend on his organization, or the mode in which the general soul incarnates itself in him. He inclines to do something which is easy to him and good when it is done, but which no other can do. He has no rival. For the more truly he consults his own power, the more difference will his work exhibit from the work of others. His ambition is exactly proportional to his powers. The height of the pinnacle is determined by the breadth of the base. Every man has this call of the power to do something unique, and no man has any other call.

WE ARE ONE WITH THE INFINITE

It is stated in the Bible, "The call compels the answer." To what are we calling in demanding to find the right job, the right labor? Is it something external to ourselves? a particular place to work? a certain individual who can provide us with an entrée to something good? Come back to what we are: expressions of Infinite Mind. (The Infinite is all.) Hold that idea steady in consciousness and the right labor will be born. It all begins in thought. Jesus' words in Matthew 11:28 give strength to this understanding: "Come unto me all ye that labor and are heavy laden, and I will give you rest." What does this mean? *Come unto me* means to come to the consciousness of *I am one with the Infinite*. The understanding of that lifts all burdens, opens all doors, frees us from any seeming limitation, and provides sustenance for all situations. It fulfills every dream, heals all wounds, and corrects any seeming error. "Come unto me"— Come unto the I Am consciousness.

As Emerson put it so very well, "for the more truly he consults his own powers, the more difference will his work exhibit from the work of others." Each of us is unique, and that very uniquenes is always waiting for expression. The uniqueness is the special expression of Infinite Mind each of us is. Emerson goes on to say (and this is critically important to all of us):

> By doing his work he makes the need felt which he can supply, and creates the taste by which he is enjoyed. By doing his work he unfolds himself. . . . The common experience is that the man fits himself as well as he can to the customary details of that work or trade he falls into, and tends it as a dog turns a spit. Then is he a part of the machine he moves; the man is lost. Until he can manage to communicate himself to others in his full stature and proportion, he does not yet find his vocation.

What Emerson is saying is simply this: Recognize your uniqueness (individual expression of God), know that there is something "special" for you, look for dimensions beyond the immediate task (know there is something with this job that you can do uniquely), and proclaim your oneness with all men, but recognize your uniqueness within that oneness. Don't fall into the pit of merely conforming to the minimum to get the job done; look for higher possibilities and manners in which to work the job, and relate effectively (lovingly) with all those involved with you. Is that not, then, really following the Great Commandment and the second one like unto it: Love God with all your heart, with all your soul, and with all your might, and love your neighbor as yourself?

Allow yourself the freedom to become that unique specialist you were designed to be. Don't fall into the pattern of being administered unto; rather, "pick up your cross" and follow the Great Presence (the I Am) within you. Our cross is our idea of limitation—our belief that labor is nonproductive, tiresome, and unrewarding. If it is unrewarding, who proclaimed it so? If it is boring, who set that into motion? If we truly want to find fulfillment in our labor (the place fulfillment can come into form), we need to examine our attitude and recognize that *that* we can control: *that* we can change!

Let us go back again to Jesus' marvelous statement found in Matthew 16:24: "If any man will come after me, let him deny himself, and take up his cross, and follow me." Deny that you are *only* your physical being; deny that you work with a *limited* mind. These are our crosses. Pick them up ("take them out") and recognize the Great Presence (the I Am) within—this is following "me." Denying our temporal (temporary) condition as reality and accepting our divine pedigree are essential in making anything fulfilling. Put this concept into the beginning of the process for fulfillment (Thought-Action-Manifestation) and there will be fulfillment in your laboring: "I am one with the Infinite, and the Infinite is the all in all. As the Infinite's expression, I have a unique function to fulfill; I accept that (I pick up my cross), and I find the 'peace that passeth all understanding.'"

The Educated
Unenlightened

Text: "God is light and in him there is no darkness at all" (1 John 1:5).

OUR ABILITY TO COPE

Do you sometimes feel inferior, inept, or limited in your ability to cope with your personal problems, including your physical and mental health? I would suspect that most of us today feel very much in this state of consciousness from time to time. When it becomes chronic, we will find a label for it and give it further credence. Just a cursory examination of all the self-help books, columns, articles, television and radio programs will convince anyone that many, if not most, of the people in North America feel unable to find the solution to personal problems of all kinds. It is interesting how the same questions are raised time after time and even answered by the same "authorities" in the same way (sometimes they come up with something "new"); yet, the search is continued and there is still no realistic, long-lasting answer. How can this be in this enlightened age with computer and other technologies bringing forth new wonders every day?

It is due to the fact that *this is not an enlightened age at all.* It is an age of great darkness in terms of the reality of our being and our potential. Because great "possibilities" have come into the world and great technological developments have taken place, we have assumed that we are very enlightened. We probably *are* the most enlightened people in world history with regard to a limited aspect of our universe: we have come to a new understanding of space (quantum physics), which has allowed us to reach the moon and beyond; we have come into a new awareness of bacteria, cells, and atoms, and we have labeled them; we have made great strides in harnessing vast amounts of latent evergy (even at that, humanity during its entire history has not used as much energy as the sun puts out in one second!); and we have developed from existing genes new organisms which have improved animal husbandry, argriculture, and even the human physical form. The wonders that we have brought about, though, often blind us to the reality of ourselves and cause many of us to feel defeated, overwhelmed, and extremely limited.

ARE WE A PRODUCT OF OUR ENVIRONMENT?

MANY OF US feel absolutely controlled by the three "E"'s in the life of each and every one of us: education, environment, and experience. These are powerful forces, to be sure. Each has had a tremendous effect on us, but too many of us have given the three "E"'s complete control, complete dominion. Of course, in some schools of psychology, it is believed that the environment is *the* determiner of what transpires in an individual's life. (These schools include education and experience under environment.) This is an outgrowth of the Freudian understanding that in childhood the individual is truly "welded" into the pattern he will follow, especially as the child is affected by early sexual experiences. B. F. Skinner, of course, was a leading practitioner of this psychology. For many years, the dominant thinking in psychology has been that we are a product of our environment. I would have no quarrel with that concept if our *total* environment were considered: what created life in the person, what sustains life in the individual, and what potential in mind there is for every individual. The behavioral psychologists ignore what we *are* and instead focus upon what we become through environmental (behavioral) conditioning.

RELEASING OUR CREATIVE POWER

IN PSYCHOANALYSIS THE core question is always: How do we see ourself? If we don't like how we see ourself, we are taken back into childhood to see how we got to that frame of reference. No matter how long we are in psychoanalysis no permanent cure will take place until we understand our uniqueness, our creative powers, our potential. How can the total releasing of creative power be managed when we have only been referenced to past experiences?

Out of the past we gain lessons and we learn much that is helpful, but it is not out of the past alone that answers for the future will come. As St. Paul said, "Let the dead past bury its dead." This does not mean there is no role for the psychologist—there certainly is; but the role must be to give a man complete understanding of what he is—physically, mentally, and spiritually. The triumphant individual is one who has accepted all three aspects of his being and recognizes that he is first an energized (spiritual) being who expresses through a body and a mind. Note the word *triumph* (*tri*, "three"; *umph*, "greatest").

Psychology cannot claim to be a science in the same manner as medicine or the correctly labeled physical and natural sciences, although many psychologists claim it to be a science. If you doubt that I am correct on this point, please just examine the records of almost any criminal trial where insanity has been claimed as a defense. If you do, you will find eminent psychologists and psychiatrists who will claim both insanity and sanity for the same individual. Where is the "science" in such testimony? Both cannot be right when both were given the same evidence. One of the basic tenets of pure science is that, given the same set of circumstances, the same results will manifest. Obviously, this cannot be said in psychology. The only reason for dwelling at all on psychology is that many people have made it our modern-day shaman. By so doing, we have been badly misled into believing that we are very much under the control of our environment, including education and experience.

A GREATER AWARENESS

MANY PEOPLE REMAIN "unenlightened" in their ability to find joy, happiness, and health because they do not realize that they have dimensions within themselves which far transcend what has come to them—and others—through environment, education, and experience. All of our environment, experience, and education are either stepping-stones or stumbling blocks to a greater awareness and a greater releasing of the total person. It is true that some seem to have been born into an environment where self-discovery is never necessary because all creature comforts have been provided in abundance. Some are born to wealth in both money and health; some are born to families which can provide unlimited formal education; some are born into situations which make it very easy to adjust to changing circumstances. Obviously, though, many are born into the opposite situation, so it would seem that "life is not fair." In fact, that has become a rather popular statement used to excuse any type of antisocial behavior. I found this statement, which I think does a marvelous job of refuting those who say "life is not fair" and that we are "controlled by our environment":

> Take a *real* man: Cripple him and you have a Sir Walter Raleigh. Bury him in the snows of Valley Forge and you have a Washington. Have him born in abject poverty and you have a Lincoln. Throw every obstacle in his path and you have a Booker T. Washington. Load him with bitter racial prejudice and you have a [Benjamin] Disraeli. Stab him with rheumatic pains until for years he cannot sleep without drugs and you have a [Charles] Steinmetz. Make him a second fiddler in an obscure South American orchestra and you have an [Arturo] Toscanini. Real men accept hardship and difficult situations as challenges. They *believe* there is something better and they can obtain it. They expand their vision beyond what is in present circumstances.
>
> *Author unknown*

It is interesting to note how few they are who have been born with "a silver spoon in the mouth" and have also made a real contribution to the betterment of mankind. Could it be that the environment was too "easy" for them to make an effort to create, to develop, to come into new understanding? Could this be what is meant by the biblical statement "It is easier for a camel to pass through the eye of a needle than for a rich man to enter the kingdom of Heaven"? It is in the *knowing* that there is a greater potential, a greater possibility, that the effort is made. The brain is a "goal-striving mechanism," as the late Dr. Maxwell Maltz said, and we give into our thought-world all of our attitudes, all of our beliefs, and all of our understanding. If that input is a consciousness of limitation, and only of the past, there is no meaningful goal. Hope is the "carrot" that allows us to find a meaningful goal. Without hope, there is no meaningful future.

BECOME MORE ENLIGHTENED

NO ONE WOULD be so foolish as to deny the importance of education, but too often the real meaning of education is forgotten. The genesis of the word from the Latin will give us a very effective clue as to what is lacking in much of today's education. The word *education* comes from the Latin *educare*, which means to pull out from within. Are we not doing too much "stuffing" and too little "pulling" in our educational systems and institutions today? It is great to know what the world has revealed, but it is just as great, or even greater, to know that there is much more to be revealed and that we are the only means through which it can come into form. A favorite biblical passage of mine is found in the words of St. Paul when speaking to the Romans (8:19): "The creation waits with eager longing for the revealing of the sons of God." What a magnificent statement with regard to becoming more enlightened!

Scientists today agree that nothing new "in its essence" has been brought forth in the universe since creation took place. True, all is evolving, changing, and shifting, but always working with the same materials. Only ideas are changing. There is nothing in the semi-conductor, the transistor, or in the television set that was not here five, ten, fifteen, or thirty million years ago. Only the ideas of man have changed—moved into new dimensions—and brought forth from that "essence" new forms, new conditions, and new matter.

Note the last clause in that magnificent statement of Paul: "revealing of the sons of God." Yes, the creation is waiting for its unfoldment, but it depends upon our recognition of what we are; it depends on our faith, our hope, that there are other possibilities than that which are already here in form. The "enlightened" individual accepts that hope and brings even more light into the world. This enlightenment has nothing to do necessarily with the individual's past experiences, environment, and education (although all could be helpful). Thomas Alva Edison, Charles Proteus Steinmetz, Nikola Tesla, and many others certainly did not have the environment that allowed them the type of hope which would permit their great revelations. They had to find some inner resource which allowed them to realize a great dream, and this resource transcended their environment, education, and experience.

Albert Einstein once made the statement that "a fact is truth qualified to a certain level of consciousness." As our consciousness (awareness) of our potential changes, we become enlightened, and we bring forth the new manifestation—we change "facts." As Einstein developed his famous theory, he made quite a point that "all is relative to something else." The greatest relativity for each and every human being is his relationship to the Universe—his recognition of his God-like nature to create, to bring forth all possibilities in his life. How wonderful it would be if we would think of ourselves as human beings in this way: human—*man hued* from the consciousness of God. This concept would bring great enlightenment!

Carl Gustav Jung wrote so convincingly of our unenlightened state when he said:

> [Contemporary man] is blind to the fact that, with all of his rationality and efficiency, he is possessed by "powers" that are beyond his control. His gods and demons have not disappeared at all; they have merely got new names. They keep him on the run with restlessness, vague apprehensions, psychological complications, an insatiable need for pills, alcohol, tobacco, food—and above all, an impressive array of neuroses.

St. Paul said much the same thing in 2 Corinthians 4:4: "Their unbelieving minds are so blinded by the god of this passing age, that the gospel of the glory of Christ, who is the very image of God, cannot dawn upon them and bring them light."

OUR BELIEF SYSTEM

I BELIEVE THESE "gods of the passing age" and the "powers beyond our control" are primarily our faulty belief system concerning ourself: what we are and of what we are a part. We have studied a great deal about what is out of order rather than about what is in order; we are much more concerned with the nature of illness than with the nature of health; we have placed our educational structure at the disposal of educators determined to find ways to bend individuals to conformity (a conformity established by the educators themselves) instead of helping the individual to understand that he or she is an individual (undivided from an Infinite Intelligence, but unique and creative); we have built stereotyped images that we are to follow regardless of whether these "images" are happy, productive, loving people (note the preoccupation with the "imaging" of television, film, sports, and even political figures), attempting to educate people to "clone" themselves into these stereotypes; and we have been teaching that only material wealth brings joy to the heart (despite overwhelming evidence that that is not the case). These are the "gods of the passing age."

THE MEANING OF RELIGION

ORGANIZED RELIGION HAS for the most part been very busy doing its utmost to develop negative self-images and hamper the creativity of the individual. Dwelling on the Book of

Leviticus (and only a small part of it that conforms to some minister's or priest's preconceived notion, it might be added) and making normal feelings seem evil, many churches have long lists of "sins" and all types of "thou shalt nots" and very little of the glory of the human, which is God's greatest achievement and handiwork. It is as George Bernard Shaw once stated: "The only trouble with Christianity is that it has never been tried." (The same could be said of Buddhism, Judaism, and all the others, for that matter.) It is strange how religions have forgotten the very meaning of *religion*, which is to make man more conscious of his relationship to Infinite Mind and Infinite Intelligence. The word *religion* comes from the Latin meaning "to bind." Instead of being bound to the nature of Infinite Mind, we are being bound to limited ideas, limited possibilities—bound to some interpretations of scripture which are highly suspect (and changed numerous times, it might be added) and to a very limited idea of what we can do and why we should do it.

We hear many people saying that the Bible in its entirety is the very word of God. If this is so, then God changed His mind many times (various translations) and was a rather poor historian for a rather small part of the world. There is no question that the Bible is a marvelous statement of the possible unfoldment of our consciousness from the wrathful, vengeful, judgmental God of the Old Testament to the loving, freeing God of much of the New Testament. It is a marvelous directory of how to grow in mind. But many of the clergy have decided to take certain passages and certain books and place their emphasis on a doomsday religion and a wrathful God. Probably the most important misunderstanding in the Christian teaching has been to assign the "Christ" to be possible to one person only: Jesus.

JESUS THE MAN / JESUS THE CHRIST

IT IS MOST difficult to go back in Church history and ascertain just when Jesus alone became the Christ. Certainly, it isn't that way in scripture, although some do translate it in that manner. This worshiping of Jesus is destroying man and Christianity. Not for a moment would I argue that Jesus did not become the Christ. I feel that he certainly did, and he deserved to be identified as the Christ; but the important point for those wishing enlightenment is to realize that he did not claim that he alone was the Christ. He knew his identity, and he proclaimed it for all humankind. He gave us the method of becoming enlightened, but he never said that enlightenment could come only through worshiping the physical Jesus.

This is *our* idea—that Jesus alone was or could be the Christ—and it has made it almost impossible for the thinking individual to accept the great truths that were given by Jesus. It is true that Jesus gave us a pattern for living which would enlighten, and thereby enrich, our entire being, but many people cannot accept the pattern because it has been related to one physical man. It is as though Jesus was never of blood and bone and never had the problems and obstacles that are commonplace to us all. We have made the physical Jesus into our God and thereby we have removed a meaningful relationship with what he taught.

This poem by Harold Emory Mason, a retired attorney and former assistant minister of the Bruen Chapel United Methodist Church, tells the story of the *real* Jesus and the *real* Christ so very well:

The Christ in Us

For generations man misunderstood
The name of Christ and used it where he would;
As Jesus Christ a surname became,
The Christ, as just a title, meant the same.

No matter how or when the name appeared
To Jesus only was distinction geared;
No other was "begotten Son of God"
Regardless of the righteous path he trod.

To date no records tell of anyone
As much entitled to be called God's son
As Jesus who did emulate Him more
And thus became the Christ, the Open Door.

In fact, the Christ in Jesus was attained
By using faith in God to be ordained
To bring the truth of life as it should be
So those from evil could and should be free.

The Christ is not a person, place or thing;
It is a Principle to which to cling—
That all men, not just Jesus, are God's sons
Who can become living and God-like ones.

Yes, all are sons and therefore all are heirs
And do become joint-heirs of One who cares;
So really if we God's laws fulfill
We can, like Jesus, also do His will.

The Christ in Jesus stressed the law of Love
Descending on the man in form of dove;
In doing greater works than he has done
We must display more love for everyone.

And when we see the Christ Divinity,
Exemplifying in the trinity
Of spirit, soul and body, all as one,
The Unity of God we will have won.

The tragedy is that there is so much of the great teaching
that is completely lost to the world because of the dependence
so many theologians have placed on the physical Jesus; yet, this

was so contrary to his great teaching. We were admonished to recognize that we have the mind of Christ, that the body is the temple of the living God, that we worship in spirit and truth, and that the letter killeth.

How unpopular what I am writing is to most of the world! Many people who call themselves Christians will become angered by the very notion that I am expressing here: that Jesus was a human being who understood the Law of Being, accepted it, lived it, and fulfilled it. Did he not say, "I come not to break the law but to fulfill it"? This preoccupation with the physical Jesus is understandable, though, in many ways. We have always had difficulty accepting concepts and ideas which are not physical. We seem to reduce everything to the physical level and so become victims to that very consciousness. The physical is so very limiting—so very much rooted in "experience, education, and environment"—and few ever make the effort to transcend it.

RAISING OUR CONSCIOUSNESS

THIS IS ONE of the primary reasons that the "metaphysical" teaching has not attracted the hordes of people who are attracted to physical teaching. The metaphysical (beyond the physical) requires that the individual use his or her mind and vision, and put the law into practice. It is so easy to say, "Jesus came to save my sins" and "I love Jesus; therefore, all is okay, as my priest [or minister] told me so." It is much more difficult to lift the mind to a consciousness of the fact that we are responsible for our acts; we are the instruments through which God's creation can be revealed, and it is revealed according to our thinking. God does not condemn, condone, or accept our thinking and our acts—He is neutral—but, as with Jesus, we must accept that all that comes to us comes by virtue of our own attitudes, our own acts, our own understanding.

It is so easy to say, "It is God's will" and so much more difficult to say, "I am responsible." Yet, this acceptance of personal responsibility in all aspects is the very heart of Jesus' teaching and is the cornerstone of true understanding. Jesus taught a lesson of love (knowing the Presence of God is there no matter what the physical may indicate); he gave the Law for effective living (the Law of Nonresistance), and he demonstrated that the lesson and the Law worked. It is a perversion of the greatest lesson and the greatest Law ever given to say this could be manifest only through this one man, to make a god of him, and, by so doing, to indicate that the lesson and the Law could manifest only through him because he was uniquely the "son of God." Some will say the recognition of Jesus as a great teacher and way-shower rather than as God takes the sense of mysticism out of Christianity. I submit that it is this very "mysticism" that has made Christianity unworkable and "unlived." There is so much mysticism surrounding how the mind works, how the Law expresses itself, and how the "art of loving" frees that there is no need to place all the burden on the physical Jesus.

BECOME AWARE OF
YOUR SPIRITUAL BEING

THE DIVISIONS THAT have come into our belief systems (Judaism, Protestant and Catholic Christianity, Buddhism, Hinduism, Islamic, and a host of others) have come because we keep insisting that our particular "savior" had all the answers. We get back to personality again, and we cannot cope with comparing the various personalities. An examination of each of the principal religions of the world indicates a great deal more sameness than difference. The startling differences (over which wars have been fought) relate to the personality (the physical being) of the particular leader. All of the great leaders whose work founded various religions admonished us to become aware of the *true* self—the spiritual being—and to let the physical "self" pass on. "Greater things than I have done you shall do" were the words of Jesus. The Buddha said almost the identical words, as did Muhammad, Krishna, and others. Yet, most of the followers of these great teachers have made a god of their leader and have become much more occupied with the individual's physical life (including where he lived) than with what the master was really telling them (witness the battle over the "physical" Jerusalem, Mecca, and other so-called holy places).

Real freedom requires that we come into the consciousness of the Presence of God in each individual and realize that each of us is responsible for the "works" of that Presence. We become "the enlightened educated" rather than "the educated unenlightened" when we recognize that God created all of humankind in His image and that we are responsible for bringing forth in our life our "God-nature" according to our belief—regardless of education, environment, and experience. Perhaps more attention should be given to this wonderful statement (Ps. 116:16): "Thou hast loosed my bonds," and the wonderful Proverb (23:7): "For as he thinketh in his heart, so is he."

You Are Not the Guilty Party

HAVE YOU EVER THOUGHT, "I am a bad person," "I am sick," "I am stupid," or "I am guilty of this or that transgression"? I doubt if any of us has not had such ideas, and those ideas have sometimes grown, festered, and caused the "real self" no end of difficulties. But the *real* you is not guilty of any transgression and has never experienced illness, lack, hatred, hunger, lack of companionship, or poverty. The *real* you knows only abundance, health, friendship, love, and understanding. The *real* you is a spiritual being—"before Abraham was, I am"—and you were never ill and never experienced any lack. The I Am—the Spirit which you are—has always been and always will be, and the I Am is guilty of nothing—has no part in it.

Now, through the housing of yourself (the body, the temple of the living God), many limiting conditions appear to have arisen. In your mind (note: *your mind*), many limiting ideas, concepts, and activities have occurred. But the *real* you is guilty of no wrongdoing.

WHAT IS GUILT?

THROUGH THE UNDERSTANDING of what I Am comes freedom from all concepts of guilt. Guilt is probably the greatest problem with which we have to contend. We feel unworthy, unclean, unhealthy, and undeserving. It is from this concept of guilt that many religions, especially Christianity, accepted the idea of Original Sin. It is, and always has been, the notion that we are physical beings and that what our eyes see, what our ears hear, what our fingers touch, what our nose smells, and what our mouth tastes are the truth of our world. This is utter nonsense! All of these things are reactions in some way to how we conceive the Truth of ourselves. Every sense (each of the five physical senses) changes when the consciousness of what I Am changes.

Of all of our problems and our feelings of unhappiness, none quite compares with the crushing weight of guilt. Psychologists, psychiatrists, and spiritual teachers all agree on one thing: the greatest problem we have to overcome is a feeling of guilt. It is rare to find anything concerning which all psychologists, psychiatrists and spiritual teachers agree, but certainly in regard to guilt there is no argument: it is our greatest problem and the greatest cause of unhappiness. It is the demoralizing, limiting, counterproductive aspect of consciousness. Guilt always creates a feeling of "unworthiness," limitation, crisis, poor self-image, and a propensity to illness.

The question needs to be asked: "What is guilt?" It is, quite obviously, a consciousness that something that was said, done, or thought was wrong, "evil," and that there is no way to get rid of it. It is a feeling of sorrow or of pity for what we assisted in having transpire. In its basic nature, too, it is a feeling that we can do nothing to correct the action and that, therefore, we are beyond redemption. Guilt creates the illusion that "I am what I did."

Individuals have spent thousands of dollars with psychologists or similar analysts in attempting to locate where, within their consciousness, the concept of guilt arose and to reveal the situation where guilt first came into "belief" for them. Psychology works on the assumption that to identify a problem is to solve the problem, or, at least, is the first step to solving it. This is a helpful concept, and it does assist one to know why one is "feeling guilty"; but it rarely provides a permanent solution, and it rarely frees the individual to build a totally new self-image.

WE CONFORM TO THE IMAGE WE HOLD

THE BASIC FEELING that arises when any guilt is present is an idea of condemnation. When we feel under condemnation, we accept the condemnation as the truth of ourself; therefore, we must think, act, and manifest whatever the condemnation has been stating. Hence, condemnation—the parent of all guilt—can come in many forms. If we have been told we are ugly, if we believe we are stupid, if we accept the concept that we cannot accomplish what we desire, we shall be under condemnation to those very things. We shall have to overcome them by recognizing that that is not the total truth of the situation. Guilt, which has come into the consciousness through condemnation, has to be "exorcised" in some way or we will conform to whatever has been established in our mind. We always conform to the image we hold, and if that image has been created through the acceptance of condemnation (guilt), we will conform to it. This is a law of mind, and there is no escaping it. If we believe that we are ugly, either mentally or physically, we will behave accordingly; we are under condemnation to the concept, hence guilt-laden, so we will conform.

As in all psychological problems, Jesus was the master

teacher. No story in modern psychology and no textbook has ever given such a basic lesson in dissolving guilt as Jesus gave in the story involving the woman found in adultery. As the story unfolded in the gospel of John, Jesus came upon men who were planning to stone the woman to death for having committed adultery. He said that he who was without sin should cast the first stone, and they all slipped away. This part of the story is very well known, but few have given proper weight to the next statement of Jesus: "Has no one condemned you?" She answered, "No one, as yet, master." Jesus said, "Nor do I condemn you; go forth and sin no more."

THE *I AM* NEVER CONDEMNS

IN THIS STATEMENT, Jesus was recognizing the truth of condemnation. He knew that if the woman believed she was an adulteress she would remain in that "image" until somehow she had expiated the feeling of guilt. He knew that to condemn her would create a self-image for her of a guilty person who was unable to lift her consciousness out of the sin of adultery and that she would remain an adulteress—she would identify with the limitation, and the guilt would "infect" her thought toward her true being. He first asked, "Who has condemned you?" And when she replied, "No one," he said, "Nor do I." He made certain that others had not condemned her and then made certain she understood that neither did he. The "I" (the I Am) never condemns. He clearly told her that what she had done was wrong, but he told her she could go—"go forth and sin no more."

He freed her from the limitation of guilt. He did not say that what she had done was right; quite the contrary. But he allowed her to see that she was not, in essence, what she had done. This is the only long-range, effective manner in which guilt can be dissolved: to realize that we make mistakes, we do things which we should not—but that is not the truth of ourselves. The truth is that we are expressions of God, unique expressions; we are one with our Parent. Though our "sins be as scarlet," we are not under permanent condemnation. The loving Father will always forgive a contrite heart.

The greatest gift that Jesus gave to man is the understanding of the forgiving, loving nature of the Father (the Omnipresence, the I Am Presence). The very word *salvation* explains the nature of God's willingness to lift all consciousness of guilt—condemnation. The preferred meaning for me of the word *salvation* is freedom from clinging to the phenomenal world of appearance and reunion with ultimate reality. The more mundane meaning of *salvation* is to reclaim, bring back into usable form. Both are excellent explanations of what happens when one dissolves guilt, and this was the greatest of all the messages of Jesus. He freed us from clinging to the phenomenal world through the Truth of ourselves and allowed us to reunite with ultimate reality.

RISE TO THE CONSCIOUSNESS OF TRUTH

How CAN ONE possibly be free to grow, to be happy, to develop, and to overcome the vicissitudes of the world when one is feeling guilty? One simply cannot! The guilt will always come forth and say, "This is what you are." Through many parables, examples, and demonstrations, Jesus explained the Truth—the act is not the actor. This he did with the woman caught in adultery. He said her act was wrong but that she could go forth and be her true self. He freed her from clinging to the phenomenal world (adultery) and allowed her to go forth with the feeling that "this act is not me." Hence, she had the opportunity to find the "ultimate reality." He truly saved her from a life of hopeless despondency, limitation, and complete sin. He allowed her to build a new image—a new, realistic self. This we all can do if we rise to the consciousness of the Truth concerning what we are and of what we are a part. No matter what we have done, how often we have done it, or how sinful it may have been, we can, with a contrite heart, be received back by the Omnipresence with open arms.

Even from a scientific approach concerning what is known of energy, the freedom to reestablish perfection is always available. When a circuit has been cut and the manifestation is no longer possible (such as a "live" line which may have fallen), once the receiver from the source is reestablished, the energy is always there ready to produce. In fact, the source of the current was always producing, but somehow the receiver had been put out of operation. Once the transmission line is reestablished and the "receiver" is again functional, the energy will come flowing through. The analogy of the clogged carburetor could be used. Once the clog in the carburetor is removed, the motor can return to its perfect functioning. However, the receiver must always be established, and the line to the receiver must be open.

OUR SOURCE OF GOOD
IS ALWAYS THERE

So, too, with ourself. Our Source of all good, all energy, all that makes for growth in all ways is always there waiting and always available with unlimited good. As the great physicist Max Planck (father of the Quantum Theory) has stated, "We live in the midst of a universal stream of energy without limit." This energy is always there waiting for us. It comes to us through the consciousness of what I am and of what I am a part. It cannot flow to us and do its good work when we are filled with feelings of guilt; this concept of guilt denies, in the most vigorous manner possible, our Source and our being part of that Source. It denies the I Am Presence, the Omnipresence, within. In accepting guilt, we fail to recognize the forgiving nature of God, the Omnipresence. Yet, the heart of the story Jesus both told and demonstrated was the forgiving, loving nature of God. How well Jesus understood that we cannot live in the concept of guilt and truly become a receiver of the good that is intended for us!

FREE YOURSELF FROM GUILT

ONE COULD WELL ask, "Well, even understanding the nature of forgiveness and the problem with condemnation, how do I free myself from guilt when I know I did wrong and sometimes I may even see the fruits of my wrongdoing?" This, of course, is the heart of our great dilemma: We know we should not accept guilt and that it is destroying us, but we can see no way of not accepting the consequences of our thinking and doing. To resolve this greatest of all problems, we must first realize that guilt is not solved by denying the guilt but by denying the concept of "I am a bad person." Hopefully, we will always recognize and realize that there are certain basic moral laws that all of us know instinctively and must obey. Many say that morals are just a case of time and geography. This is utter nonsense. To be sure, there are laws that we make to enforce our ideas of morality, but these are not the concepts that give us guilt feelings. In all races, all cultures, at all times, there are certain concepts and acts that are known instinctively to be wrong—that are sins (limitations). Unfortunately we have added so many "man-made" laws to these basic, intrinsically understood moral laws that there can be some confusion.

But, basically, we know when we are doing that which is not

moral. Once we understand that these basic laws are designed for our own good and for our own growth, we will rarely break them. However, if we do we shall see that we have broken a moral law; it should be a fairly easy step to the realization that we can do nothing about what we did, but the experience has taught us what not to do in the future. We can turn what could easily become a ''guilt'' feeling into a growth experience. This we do by divorcing completely the concept of the act being the actor. The actor learns through playing his role, as we all do. Sometimes society must make certain that we have learned through the role experience. Hence, society often imposes penalties, punishment, and incarceration to make certain the experience is understood.

All civilized law is based on the premise of the act perhaps being wrong but not the actor. We don't penalize people for being people; we may have to discipline them for what they have done.

WE MUST FORGIVE OURSELVES AND OTHERS

THE BASIC STEP, then, in dissolving guilt is to realize that what one has done may be in error but that it is not the Truth of one's being. Error is never Truth and cannot become Truth, no matter how many times it is made or how vehemently affirmed. Error is always a lie and an abomination. When we think of ourself as the wicked deed we performed, we are lying to ourself and destroying ourself (bearing false witness). We must learn to forgive ourself if we are to dissolve guilt—singly or collectively. Collective guilt feelings, many psychologists and spiritual students feel, is Americans' number-one problem. However, whether guilt feelings are single or collective, they are giving power to a lie and an abomination. Certainly what was done may have been wrong; but as long as one holds to the condemnation of being a wrongdoer, that is what one must become. As Shakespeare put it (paraphrased), "To err is human, to forgive is divine." Shakespeare was not eliminating self-forgiveness from this powerful Truth statement. As in the great Lord's Prayer, "Forgive us our trespasses as we forgive others." The key, of course, is that we find our freedom from guilt when we quit condemning others. Total forgiveness is all-important.

A HIGHER MORAL CODE

FEELINGS OF GUILT indicate that we are recognizing two very limiting ideas: that we cannot overcome what we have done and that we must live under the penalty of condemnation. The feeling of guilt also indicates one very healthy concept we have: that there is a higher moral code than we have been observing. To dissolve guilt, emphasis must be placed on the healthy concept of a higher moral code than is present in our mind, and the elimination of the belief in limitation and non-forgiveness. When we recognize that there is a higher level of morality than we have as yet recognized, we are then forced to recognize, if we are logical, that there is order in the universe and that we can understand that order. This implies, at least, the existence of an Omnipresent Power, Intelligence, in the universe. When one comprehends this, one is not far from beginning to understand that with order in the universe there had to be a Creator (the creation proves the existence of a Creator). When one understands, or at least has a "glimmer" of, a Creator, one is then on the way to really dissolving one's guilt. The Creator, who made all in perfection, would not want to see Its creation held in imperfection.

CULTIVATE A NEW
CONSCIOUSNESS

THE NEGATIVE CONCEPTS that the "guilty feeling" person has make very fertile grounds for cultivating an entirely new consciousness. The feeling that one cannot overcome is a denial of the God Presence and is giving power to a lie. When we say that we cannot overcome, we are saying that the power in the limited situation is greater than the power in perfection. We are recognizing the limitation as the Truth, and as long as that concept is held, we will hold to our guilt feelings. When we are allowed to see the perfection in which the Creation stands, the scientific verification of the latent potential in our brain alone, we should begin to comprehend that our feeling of "I cannot" is not true. "Living in the Omnipresent" is another way of saying "living in the present with the consciousness of the I Am (Omnipresence, God)." To lift the consciousness in regard to what I am and of what I am a part is the only way to start living in the Omnipresence. When we recognize what we are (an emanation of God, a child of God), we shall know that we can overcome. The closer we come to a complete awareness of the Presence of God, the closer we shall come to the dissolution of guilt. Once we know that we are one with the Omnipresence, the feeling of unforgiveness lifts. A feeling of guilt and an awareness of the Omnipresence cannot be felt at the same time, and an awareness of the Omnipresence brings a certainty of forgiveness. The presence of guilt must be evidence of the absence of a consciousness of the I Am Presence.

For thousands of years various learned individuals—priests, alchemists, soothsayers, augerers, psychologists—have wrestled with freeing humankind from guilt feelings. Sometimes this is called exorcising and sometimes psychoanalysis. But the quest is the same: how to help us comprehend that what we believe we are, we become. If we hold that we are alone, that we have no Source, that we came into creation through an accidental explosion with no origination, and that there is nothing for us but our present expression here on earth, then we shall necessarily be full of guilt feelings (and many other types of limited concepts). We shall be forced into many guilty ideas because our instinctive nature still tells us that certain thoughts and acts are wrong. We shall continue to hold onto the concept that we are what the act is, and there will be little mental or physical health in us. We will hold that evil—falsity—is Truth, and we shall be chained to that concept. Only through the consciousness of the One Presence and One Power will this enchainment be broken.

RECOGNIZING YOUR SOURCE

For more than eighty years humankind has been highly involved with psychoanalysis and various psychological studies. We are told that mental illness is on the rise and that never before have so many of us felt condemned by guilt complexes and feelings. We have had affirmed to us over and over again that our pace of living is causing our increased mental breakdown and that self-condemnation (disguised through ideas of failure and comparing one with another) is on the increase. I believe that the "pace of living" today has very little to do with the mental difficulties that are rampant. Rather, I believe the cause rests in our failure to recognize our Source and the unlimited potential we have through that Source.

It is through the preoccupation with such pseudo sciences as psychology and sociology that we are increasingly unable to relate effectively to society. Where in the typical psychological jargon does one find reference to the One Presence? Where is the understanding of the forgiving nature of that Presence? Where is the explanation of our unlimited capacity? We keep trying to solve our guilt problems through attacking all forms of discipline, especially self-discipline, through an emphasis on the negative work and activities done by some groups; through attacking, as though in the name of Truth, everything that is believed to be out of order in the world. The answer is found through becoming a disciple to the Christ (the I Am)—disciplined to the Presence within. (As Jesus said to Andrew, "Come with me and be fishers of men.")

This tremendous, massive, collective, and personal guilt feeling rampant in our society today will never be solved through the pseudo sciences of psychology and sociology, or, at least, as those so-called disciplines are now understood. Despite the scoffing of those who, in their ignorance, have not studied Truth, the basic understanding of guilt and how to overcome it will be found by an increasing awareness of the spiritual nature of humanity and how that nature is activated, enlarged, and increased. We are going to have to reclaim our true nature—our spiritual nature—or we shall be increasingly caught up in concepts of guilt. We shall have to renounce (rename) our dependency on the physical (material) aspects of ourself and our world to be free of the guilt that is now creating such havoc in us individually and in society collectively. We shall have to reclaim (salvage) our birthright as a unique, divine expression of God or we shall continue to live in the mire of all of the limitations imposed through belief in guilt.

LOVE GOD WITH ALL YOUR MIND, HEART, AND SOUL

JESUS "SAVED US" through his thought, action, and manifestation as an expression of God, and he claimed that same manifestation for all of us. He gave us wonderful, practical, and beautiful parables and stories concerning our birthright and our inheritance. All of these great stories and demonstrations are centered on the concept of the One Presence and the One Power which is all-forgiving, all-loving, and always accessible with unlimited abundance. He even gave us the principle law by which to live: Love God with all your heart, soul, and mind.

Yes, guilt can be dissolved, and it is not an impossible task. The words of the Nazarene who became the Christ are completely applicable and should be the one principle we hold when we feel oppressed by guilt; and these words, if believed, will free us:

> In very truth I tell you if you ask the Father for anything in my name, he will give it you (John 16:23).

> But the time approaches, indeed it is already here, when those who are real worshippers will worship the Father in spirit and in truth. Such are the worshippers whom the Father wants. God is spirit, and those who worship him must worship in spirit and in truth (John 4:23,24).

Your Own "Open Sesame"

The Arabian Nights tales, the many Arthurian stories, and many of the great Aesop fables have some kind of magic wand in their stories—more likely a magic word—which opens the gates to plenty, to complete peace and security. Probably the most popular is the statement, "Open sesame!" It appears in *Ali Baba and the Forty Thieves*. As you may recall the story, whenever Ali Baba wanted to enter the chamber of great wealth that was always barred to others, he used the magic words, "Open sesame!"

YOUR OWN STATEMENT OPENS DOORS TO ABUNDANCE

I imagine that when you were a child this story fascinated you, and you wondered if there wasn't some magic statement you could make which would open closed doors for you.

How great it is to know that every individual has just such a statement available to him, and it is in his own private code; that is, no one can use it for his good except the individual himself. Every individual has his own statement which opens doors to abundance, and it is buried in his subconscious. It is a very simple statement—as simple as "Open sesame!"—but it is of no value until it is recognized and utilized. "Open sesame!" did Ali Baba no good until he recognized that it had value and then put it into use.

This, of course, is true of all things. Nothing has any value until it is recognized as valuable; gold, diamonds, emeralds, and platinum had no value until humankind recognized them as valuable. We can "de-recognize" them at any time, and they become valueless. So, too, was the situation with Ali Baba. However, recognition of value remains of no worth until it is placed into use. The fact that Ali Baba knew the words were valuable was of no worth to him until he used them—until he spoke the words. In our own world the "open sesame" is a very simple word, but it must be given value and be put to use with the right understanding. That word is *thanks*. *Thanks* is our "open sesame" to the riches of love, joy, plenty, understanding, happy relationships, and increase in all good things.

THE GOOD HAS BEEN THERE ALL THE TIME

WHAT IS THE "magic"—the magic wand—which lies in this marvelous word *thanks*? Basically, when *thanks* is used with deep emotional feeling and comprehension, it verifies that the good has been there for us all the time and has now been "opened" to us through a certain channel. Sometimes that channel for our good has been a particular person or group of persons. We acknowledge their instrumentality for our good by saying, "thanks." Some say this is simply common courtesy, and that is true; but it is a small part of the real reason for affirming our gratitude by expressing thanks. The very basis of our future good and of even enjoying the "now" is to speak the word *thanks* with meaning, vigor, and understanding. By speaking the word, we have reaffirmed and confirmed that the channel for our good is always open if we are receptive. Receptivity requires acknowledgment of a source; we keep the source open through the confirmation—by thanks.

In confirming by thanking, we have had to reach into the subconscious mind and acknowledge that our good—our plenty —was there waiting for us. We have had to "program" ourselves to an awareness that there are many channels through which our good can come to us. We have given value to an underlying principle of good—the knowledge of a greater potential than that which had hitherto been expressed. It is put as follows in Proverbs 3:6: "In all thy ways acknowledge him." There is no greater way of acknowledging the presence of an Infinite, Loving God than to express *thanks* to whatever channel has brought forth a bit of the Infinite Source's abundance to us.

CONFIRMING AND REAFFIRMING THE INFINITE SOURCE OF GOOD

IT WAS MOST interesting when studying the history of the Founders of the United States to recognize how completely they understood the essential nature of confirming and reaffirming the Infinite Source of good. It was by mere chance—or politics—that a day was established in which to acknowledge the presence of abundance. (Even before our nation was established, the Pilgrims knew this great secret, "open sesame," to their good.) It would be wise for us to study the first Thanksgiving Proclamation, which was made by President George

Washington on October 3, 1789 (and please note the overwhelming acknowledgment of the Source of all good which we call God):

Whereas, it is the duty of all nations to acknowledge the providence of Almighty God, to obey His will, to be grateful for His benefits, and humbly to implore His protection and favor; and

Whereas, both Houses of Congress have, by their joint committee, requested me to recommend to the people of the United States a day of public thanksgiving and prayer, to be observed by acknowledging with grateful hearts the many and signal favors of Almighty God, especially by affording them an opportunity peacefully to establish a form of government for their safety and happiness:

Now, therefore, I do recommend and assign Thursday, the 26th Day of November next, to be devoted by the people of these States to the service of that great and glorious Being who is the beneficent author of all the good that was, that is, or that will be; that we may then all unite in rendering unto Him our sincere and humble thanks for His kind care and protection of the people of this country previous to their becoming a nation; for the signal and manifold mercies and the favorable interpositions of His providence in the course and conclusion of the late war; for the great degree of tranquility, union, and plenty which we have since enjoyed; for the peaceable and rational manner in which we have been enabled to establish constitutions of government for our safety and happiness, and particularly the national one now lately instituted; for the civil and religious liberty with which we are blessed, and the means we have of acquiring and diffusing useful knowledge; and, in general, for all the great and various favors which He has been pleased to confer upon us.

And also that we may then unite in most humbly offering our prayers and supplications to the great Lord and Ruler of Nations, and beseech Him to pardon our national and other transgressions; to enable us all, whether in public or private stations, to perform our several and relative duties properly and punctually; to render our National Government a blessing to all the people by constantly being a Government of wise, just, and constitutional laws, discreetly and faithfully executed and obeyed; to protect and guide all sovereigns and nations (especially such as have shown kindness to us), and to bless them with good government, peace, and concord; to promote the knowledge and practice of true religion and virtue, and the increase of science among them and us; and, generally, to grant unto all mankind such a degree of temporal prosperity as He alone knows to be best.

Given under my hand, at the city of New York, the 3rd Day of October A.D. 1789.

—George Washington

In even a cursory reading and examination of this Proclamation, it is obvious that the first Congress and first President knew where their Source of supply was, and they were more than willing to acknowledge it, knowing full well that the act —which had to be worked out through the collective consciousness—was a necessity for the continual prosperity and general good of the counrty.

GIVING THANKS FOR
THE PRESENCE

THE FOUNDERS DID not see any conflict between science and religion (a belief in One Presence and One Power). Note that in the Proclamation religion and science are both mentioned in the same clause: "to promote the knowledge and practice of true religion and virtue, and the increase of science among them and us." This acknowledgment of the relationship between religion and science and the expression of thanks with regard to the gift of both is one of the very cornerstones of the building of America. *It was the "thank you" that made it firm in the conscious and subconscious mind of early leaders.*

Perhaps we should give a glance at why our country prospered so mightily, given the current crusade against any public acknowledgment of the Presence of One Provider. (The Proclamation stated: "It is the duty of all nations to acknowledge the providence of Almighty God, to obey His will, to be grateful for His benefits, and humbly to implore His protection and favor . . . to recommend to the people of the United States a day of public thanksgiving and prayer, to be observed by acknowledging with grateful hearts the many and signal favors of Almighty God.")

Through this Proclamation, through the Constitution, and through the Declaration of Independence, one can easily see that the very foundation of this nation was based on the recognition of the Almighty Presence and giving thanks for the Presence.

What is our own experience? Have we given thanks for the fact of life? for the many bountiful good and goods that we have? for the loving friends and relatives? for the opportunity to express ourselves at "our level" of consciousness? for our jobs and other sources of income? It is not too difficult to give thanks for these obvious treasures that are in our lives. But what about the negative situations, people, conditions, and circumstances in our world? Have we given thanks for them? Most people would feel that this would only confirm these negative conditions. But how do we find the "open sesame" to move beyond condition and circumstance?

I don't mean to imply that we should give thanks specifically for these negative situations in our lives, but it is essential that we give thanks for the Presence of the Omnipresence (the I Am) *despite appearances of negativity*. The Pilgrims rightly gave thanks their first year in the New World despite almost desperate conditions and circumstances that prevailed. What were they doing? *They were affirming and confirming the Presence of God in their lives, which opened the door to their subconscious where the answers to their problems existed.*

THE UNLIMITED TREASURE WITHIN OURSELVES IS OPENED

THROUGHOUT SCRIPTURE THE "open sesame" of thanks is to be found. "We are bound always to thank God" (2 Thess. 2:13); "Thanks be to God who gives us the victory" (1 Cor. 15:57); "Thanks be unto God for his unspeakable gift" (2 Cor. 9:15). Each of these statements deserves our very close attention as each confirms that it is through the giving of thanks that the door to the unlimited treasure within ourselves is opened. Giving thanks is truly our "open sesame" for all of the abundance that is of this world.

A number of the founders—and slightly later Daniel and Noah Webster—placed a great deal of emphasis on the importance of celebrating as a nation a day of thanksgiving. What was carried on was often based on the scripture found in the writings of Paul, especially chapter 9 of 2 Corinthians. Among other passages are these: "Being enriched in every thing to all bountifulness, which causeth through us thanksgiving to God. For the administration of this service not only supplieth the want of the saints, but is abundant also by many thanksgivings unto God" (2 Cor. 9:11,12).

GIVING THANKS

TITHING WAS ALSO very much in the minds and hearts of the early founders of this nation—not the rigidity of giving to a specific organization and to the giving of money alone, but the "tithing" of giving thanks, of spending time in prayer and contemplation of the nature of God within us. It is interesting how many in this world tithe "religiously" of their money income and ignore perhaps the most important aspect of tithing—to give of *time* to praise God and to give thanks. If we gave one tenth of our time (144 minutes per day) to thanking the Infinite Presence for our good, we would change our world almost immediately for the better.

I don't mean by this that 144 minutes should be spent in quiet with emphasis only on biblical statements or on so-called spiritual things; true thanks expressed through tithing of time could involve enjoying the beauty of God's creation, expressing gratitude to those around us, giving thanks for the wonders and marvels of nature. In all of this we would purify our consciousness and allow the wonderful presence of the I Am to flow more fully through us. Giving thanks through tithing could be done, at least in part, through the wonderful practice advocated by Isaiah: "In quietness and confidence is thy strength" (Isaiah 30:15).

The great master psychiatrist Dr. Carl Jung said there can be no problem without consciousness. If our consciousness is constantly focused on giving thanks for the Presence of God in us, there is no room for the problem. Conditions and circumstances may arise which the so-called normal man will call problems; but if we would stop our negative thinking and say, "Thank you, Father," the miracle of overcoming could and would take place. Most of us, however, start condemning the situation (problem) and, obviously, there can be no answer (you are under "condemnation" instead of the "grace" of God). The avenue to the grace (freedom, joy, forgiveness) is through thanking the Father for His Infinite Presence (the I Am).

It was not accidentally that Jesus confirmed his identity *before* he made an effort to overcome a problem. He said, "Thank you, Father." (Sometimes he said, "Abba, Father," meaning, of course, "Father, Father," which was an endearment equal to *thank you*.) Naturally, he had his miracle because he confirmed his identity as one with the Father (Source) before he acted. His consciousness, through thanks, was on his true nature (one with God), so there could be no unsolvable problem.

Identity is the key to unlocking any seeming limited situation, and there is no more effective a manner in which to identify than to give thanks for what we are; i.e., special expressions of the Infinite (I Am Presence). It is interesting that in order to enter any secret order, to move into "certain circles," one is asked to identify oneself. The key to the ultimate identification of our oneness with God is "Thank you, Father."

HAVE YOUR PERFECT DEMONSTRATION

MANY OF US CLOSE the door to our good—lose the opportunity—by failing to *always* give thanks to the Great Presence within. We thank everyone for everything—at least, some of us do—but fail to thank the Source of *all* of our good. Naturally, then, the Infinite Presence is not in mind and cannot be in form. We even have a statement that fits this perfectly:

"Out of sight, out of mind" (Arthur Hugh Clough in *Sons in Absence*). Our "sight" is not focused on giving thanks to the source, so it is not in mind, and hence cannot come to our assistance when tribulation seems to be upon us. Keep your sight on what you truly are and what made that possible, and confirm this in every possible way through thanksgiving, and you will have your perfect demonstration. There are no limits to God's possibilities, but the door through which the Infinite can work must be kept open. This is done through acknowledging the Presence with thanks.

Actually, some scientists are telling us today that giving thanks for what we are about to eat (often called *saying grace*) changes the electromagnetic impulses in the food. Nothing can remain the same when thanks, given with true understanding and feeling, is pronounced. The most powerful "door opener" ever devised, much greater than what Ali Baba possessed, is in the keeping of every one of us: it is giving thanks to our Parent with understanding, meaning, and expectation of reinforcing the Presence within. We say, and affirm, "Thank you, Father; thank you, Father; Abba, Father!"

The "Well" and the "Will"

THE TITLE OF THIS essay will cause many to wonder what it is all about—The "Well" and the "Will." I felt very strongly about picking this topic and took it from two proverbs:

Proverbs 16:22: Understanding is the wellspring of life unto him that hath it; but the instruction of fools is folly.

Proverbs 18:4: The words of a man's mouth are as deep waters; and the wellspring of wisdom as a flowing brook.

The wellspring of all life is God's ability to come forth within ourselves. The deep God feeling is the wellspring that produces the quickening within us. It is our acceptance of the wellspring within that brings God's Will into manifestation. There is an absolute relationship between the wellspring—the well, the depth of understanding—and whether we are attuned to God's Will. Our will, of course, is the will that most of us try to work with all of the time, and it is one that we *must* work with. But we must lift it up and bring it into the wellspring, endow it with the Infinite Knowledge, God knowledge, which is there within every one of us.

OUR SOURCE OF ABUNDANCE

FIRST, WE SHOULD think of how we conceive a "well." What is your concept of a well? Many think of it as a deep, bottomless pit; others see a well as a source of abundance. What we conceive stems from our own inner conviction and awareness. Do we see the well of "life" as abysmal darkness that has nothing of value for us, or do we see it as abundance for us that is waiting to spring forth—the wellspring? Do we believe a wellspring is simply a collection of ideas, concepts, rules, laws, and dogma which we have learned through education, through experiences, and through environment? Is it simply what we put in there? Then, of course, all we can take out of this wellspring is what we put in. It is like building a little fishpond or a little pool in the backyard: we must keep adding the water to it. There is no abundance, no source, except what we give to it, as contrasted to a brook or a spring—a wellspring—that is in our yard, or in our area, where fresh water comes forth. We all have the wellspring, but our opening to it depends on whether we accept that we have a tiny pool that we add to or whether we accept that we have a wellspring.

Can you visualize an inner reservoir of strength, innate intelligence, all-encompassing love? Where does a new idea come from? It certainly did not come out of the old. We may have taken the old and put it together in a new way, but it did not come *out* of the old. It came out of something within us that we often call *intuition*, meaning *in oneness*. But where did that come from? It came from within; it is the wellspring of God within us. Our understanding of our possession of a wellspring of infinite health, wisdom, and prosperity will permit us to experience those very things. But if we think it is a bottomless pit then, of course, that is what we shall experience. If there is nothing there worthwhile, then we cannot experience health, wisdom, and prosperity. There is no way in which we can. If ours is an understanding that it is only what we have placed there through external stimuli, then our wellspring has run dry and there is no help in it—there can't be, because our well now can only bring forth that which we have already put into it.

COME ALIVE TO YOUR GOOD

THAT IS WHY we say in the wonderful Lord's Prayer, "Thy will be done." Our will, our knowledge, is limited to our current state of consciousness; if we have limited our consciousness to a limited idea of the wellspring (the I Am Presence, the Omnipresence), that is all we can bring forth and we are stuck with it. Most of the world today is stuck with that very thing— what is already in manifestation. We talk about energy crisis and we have one—there is no question about it—but it is not an energy crisis so much as it is a consciousness crisis.

We are going to have one crisis after another, as we are having, and each crisis is going to become more and more severe until we become aware that the answer is not in that which is already in expression; but as we begin to hold on to a wellspring, with the knowledge that God is waiting within ourselves to become quickened and alive, we will overcome. Actually, this expression has a very deep meaning: The quick and alive are those who recognize the wellspring of God. *Quickening* meant, and still means, to become alert to truth. We come alive to all of our good, all of our abundance, by understanding that we are not controlled by external forces unless we accept them. And, of course, we can accept them. In this negative world we are living in today, many of us are caught up in this external force.

OUR UNDERSTANDING

TRULY IT IS as stated by the great words of Solomon: "Understanding is like a wellspring of life to him who hath it; but the instruction of fools is folly." Where do we get our instruction today? Many times I have gone back over my notes from when I was a student many years ago and working in psychology, and I sit back and read my material for laughs. It is absolutely hilarious. I even look back at some of my notes which I used in my classes at the university fifteen and twenty years ago, and I would, and should, be fired if I gave those same lectures today. I had to use that material; I had to state these "so-called" facts, because that was the state of truth in that very limited, nonscientific field called psychology. Almost every day we read in the newspapers where some psychologist is telling us to do this or that, and a week later some psychologist is telling us that it is going to destroy us if we do. If we follow the current "popular" psychological theory, very often we are really in trouble.

Thinking of the laetrile* controversy (and I know little about laetrile), I would say this: it is absolutely insidious that we have a few people in our government who feel they know everything about us but have based all of their studies on rats. We have also been involved in controversy over saccharin and all sorts of foods, even though biologically we know that rats are not exactly like us. But, more importantly, the rat does not have the ability to go to the wellspring and overcome. The more we have people in government and politics telling us what we can eat,

*A drug derived from apricot pits used in attempts at treating cancer.

what we can drink, and what we can wear (they are trying to dictate that too), the more we are in trouble, because we are putting our authority on man-made ideas.

I do not want to get involved politically here, but it is extremely interesting that those who call themselves confirmed liberals are the very ones who are trying to legislate what is good for us. That would be all right if they were spiritually endowed people (maybe some of them are), but understanding is the wellspring of life, and "to him that hath it shall be given." We must remember, the instruction of fools is folly. If we base our authority on anything except the truth of what we are—that we have the mind of Christ, which we must bring into a quickened and alive state—we are going to be constantly controlled by those who come along to tell us they have all the wisdom. They are the fools, and we are going to be "in folly" because we follow them.

REALIZATION OF THE CHRIST WITHIN

FROM WHAT IS our source of understanding? Where do we attain it? Are we followers of the wise men or of fools? Are we following the current rage in psychology or the current rage in political activities, or do we follow a course from the wellspring of life which is the realization of the Christ within? This is the question we must be asking ourselves, and it is becoming more important that we ask it because we are in an age of crisis. Crisis is, of course, as the Chinese word for *crisis* tells us, a problem with an opportunity. If we don't seize the opportunity in this age of crisis to change our consciousness out of the bottomless pit and accept the wellspring of the abundance of the Christ within, we are going to be in trouble.

SCIENTIFIC WISDOM

It has been fascinating to me to watch the scientific changes and claims that have come out concerning things such as laetrile and saccharin. Art Hoppe wrote in his column around the year 1988:

> There is nothing left that we can eat except seaweed; and someone discovered that there was something in seaweed that had too much iodine that killed a rat (out of a billion rats) and as a result all of mankind had to perish because the government said you can't eat anything —nothing is safe.

He ended up by saying, "Living is hazardous to your health."

This "limited idea concerning human potential" is what we are getting into more and more in our consciousness. We must come back to our wellspring, because this nation and this world are not going to survive much longer in any known form by clinging to the limited consciouness of the authorities of the scientific world. The spiritual scientist is the one that we are going to see "raise us up," as Albert Einstein did. The wise one is not the one who is purely intellectual. The wise one, the *brilliant* scientist, the real scientists such as Einstein and Wernher von Braun, have brought love into their intellect; they have given us scientific wisdom. But the scientist without the consciousness of the wellspring of God within will be leading us into folly because we will be following limited ideas, limited consciousness.

OUR WORDS REFLECT
OUR THOUGHTS

PROVERBS 18:4 TELLS us, "The words of a man's mouth are as deep waters and the wellspring of wisdom as a flowing brook." It is what comes out of our mouth that matters because it must reflect a thought that was there. This is why all religions, and even some psychologists, have told us to be very wary of blasphemy, of swearing. When you walk down the streets of a city, it is very embarrassing, especially if you are with another person, to hear the blasphemy and the swearing. We say of the use of negative words, "Oh well, they don't really mean that." But the words had to pass through their consciousness, and they are bringing forth a very limited concept. It is going to get worse and worse until there is some turning to the wellspring within. It is what comes out of the mouth that matters, because it always reflects a thought. As Jesus said, "It is not what a man puts in his mouth that matters, but what comes out." Blasphemy and swearing are denying the wellspring. Be wary of what you say. It is not a macho or "cool" thing to use foul language. In fact, it shows only ignorance—because it shows that a person has no awareness of what he is, therefore no self-respect. It is rather startling to find out that the crimes committed by women rose nearly 75 percent in the 1970s, and there are many people who have studied the situation who say that part of this was due to the fact that many women felt that in order to express their "newly liberated" womanhood, they had to use vile language. This was a false assumption and, of course, it had to come out in manifested form. We must be very careful of what comes forth from our mouths—because we have accepted it first in consciousness before it comes forth.

UNDERSTAND OUR
GOD-NATURE WITHIN

THE WORDS OF the mouth are as deep waters because through the spoken word come our conscious and subconsious thoughts, and we must be very careful to look at and examine these deep waters. Everything can be found there, and it can be handled as we determine. Everything is there but is brought forth according to what our will has been, so "well" can come into fulfillment only by our "will." When the determination is to understand our God-nature, the I Am within, then wisdom will flow continuously, just as the cool, clear water always flows in a running brook. The deep waters, of course, are not easily brought alive and quickened. The deep waters are stagnant and still until something brings them to the surface where they then become active. We bring forth the great wellspring of God whenever we "will," and our wisdom can flow as a brook whenever we "will." It is up to us what we bring forth ("to him that hath shall be given").

We have a saying, "Still waters run deep"—and we are talking about consciousness. In Titus 1:15 we read, "Unto the pure, all things are pure." Romans 14:14 states, "There is nothing unclean of itself, but to him that esteemeth anything to be unclean to him it is unclean." Along this line, Dr. Joseph Murphy, in his wonderful book *Great Bible Truths for Human Problems*, has said, "There is nothing in itself unclean. By our conception, or conceived estimate of ourselves, we see others as clean or unclean." It is the most natural thing in the world for a pear tree to bear pears, an apple tree to bear apples, and for us to mold the circumstances of our lives in harmony with our inner nature. "I am the vine, ye are the branches," as Jesus stated. A branch is rooted in the vine, and in order to change the fruit, we must change the mind. I Am, of course, is God, Being, Life, Awareness. Six-plus billion people in our world are rooted in the I Am, the wellspring, or Life Principle. Therefore they are all rooted in each of us, and each in them. By our life fruit, others bear witness to the state of consciousness in which we dwell.

WHATEVER WE ATTACH TO
I AM WE BECOME

OUR I AMness, our consciousness, is our way in which we change the world. Whatever we attach to I Am, we must become. As we affirm with feeling, "I am illumined, inspired, loving, harmonious, peaceful, happy, and strong," we begin to resurrect qualities that lie dormant within this great wellspring within us, and wonders begin to happen to us. They must! And when people help us in our realization of our dreams, they are playing their part and are messengers testifying to our beliefs, circumstances, and convictions. We wrote the play, and other men and women execute the parts conforming to our concept of ourselves.

Again, Dr. Murphy says, "It is wholly unnecessary for you to proselytize and try to make the world holy. You will not change the world that way. You will change the world when you actually become the embodiment of that which you want the world to be. Remember a very simple truth: unless you are that which you want the world to be, you will never see it in this world." You have not brought it forth in your being; therefore, it cannot be in your expression. Your expression includes everything that you visualized, everything with which you worked.

BRING FORTH THE WELLSPRING

WE ARE TOLD IN Revelation 3:8, "I have set before thee an open door and no man can shut it." But we shut it ourselves.

But don't we shut that door, saying, "Well, I can't because of this or that"? We certainly do. We shut the door. We put the trap over the well and it cannot spring forth into our being.

We come into this wellspring—these deep waters—when we understand and have an awareness that it is God's "will" that we find the "well" and all of its meaning. The "well" is Source in body and mind and in all other things. It is our will which brings forth the wellspring of our being. The "will" and the "well" are intermingled to the "nth" degree. It is wonderful to realize that we create the dream called life. There is a wonderful song, which is my favorite, entitled "The Impossible Dream." What does it tell us? To dream the impossible dream— that is our life. If the dream is that of envy and lust, of greed, of anything less than the understanding of God (we are here to glorify God—that is why we were created), if it is anything less than that in our consciousness, then our life will have to be less in expression. We are the creators of the drama called life. We are the dramatist. We are writing the most marvelous play, we are the star in it, and it is our life. Isn't that wonderful? We get to write a play, star in it, and be the only performer.

WE ARE NOT CONTROLLED

WE ARE NOT controlled, protected, or manipulated by anything that we have not created or accepted in some way. All modern-day psychology, in dealing with the psychotic, recognizes that he has accepted something as controlling him. We are *not* controlled; it is our consciousness that creates all of the outer. Even though the wellspring of perfection is there for all— all, without exception—it is our willingness to understand our nature, our oneness with the I Am, that brings the drama that is effective, happy, and complete into our lives. The wellspring of life is limited only to our perception of God, our oneness with

Creation. We may feel that mysterious forces, people, and conditions control us, but we fail to realize that our *acceptance* of these forces, people, and conditions permits them to control us.

St. Augustine, one of the greatest writers and human beings the world has ever known, lived in the fourth century. Some who have studied his life and read one of his many books, *The Confessions*, realize that this man was certainly not "good" in his youth. He was quite a rascal in many ways. He was a drug addict in a time when drug addicts were not known quite as well as they are today, a very mischievous man, a lustful man. These were physical things; in his heart he hated the bigoted and all types of human evaluation because he felt they were controlled by the powers of the government in Rome. He felt they had taken away his freedom, and he fled into what was known as Gaul at that time. He felt he was pursued there. Suddenly, as those who have read his story will remember, he realized that "the only reason I am controlled is because I accept that concept."

St. Augustine made a change. He became overwhelmingly the most popular and powerful leader at that time in a very deep spiritual sense, and there were marvelous, unbelievable things that he accomplished. He *had* accepted the authorities of the world at that time, and he was hearing things around him constantly that he felt were driving him—he accepted and believed in them—but when he no longer accepted them, he got over them and was lifted up. He was still a very human person. There is a delightful little story that he would say, "Lord, please give me chastity—but not quite yet." That was even when he was quite an elderly man. But he was still able to overcome, because he accepted the fact that there was a wellspring; there was a deepness that he had not tapped because he had always been dealing with that which he felt in his physical world with his five senses.

We must recognize that the brain is always the obedient servant of whatever it has been given through thought. The brain and the nervous system cannot tell the difference between vivid imagination and reality. The brain is the obedient servant of whatever it has been given through thought. We are not attuned to the Infinite Source if we feel controlled, driven, or limited in any manner, shape, or means. If we accept as authorities of our world those whom we might call the political, nonspiritually endowed scientists, we are going to be in deep trouble.

EXAMINE YOUR FAITH

A wonderful French lady, Grace Gassette, in her book *The Key* (which has been translated into English), states, "No philosophic system, no mental gymnastics could be applied to our daily existence if Jesus had not shown us the way, and others too." Jesus demonstrated the laws in his teachings and in his own life in a manner that could be understood by the simplest of human beings. Every man may understand the teachings of Jesus and obtain remarkable results. "To him that believeth," he has affirmed, "all things are possible." And this possibility is not reserved for some special category of human. It is the portion and privilege of all and, consequently, the privilege and portion of you yourself. God did not play favorites. The sun shines equally on the just and the unjust. Examine your faith in regard to your wellspring and you will discover why you may or may not be receiving the perfect abundance in whatever category you desire.

Does your faith in one Power, one Presence, one perfect Creator equal your faith that the sun will rise in the morning or that the highway ahead of you is clear at night? Think of the faith that we express in driving our highways. Does your faith in the One Presence equal that—or that the letter will go on its way when dropped in the letterbox? Is your faith even as great as that (limited as that might be today)? That no matter how great a drought, the rain will fall again? We all believe that. I could give

many more examples here, trying to point out that in all areas
it is our faith that allows us to proceed or not to proceed. That
is the thing that gives us the incentive to move on or not move
on. This is where we take from the wellspring of the good or
don't take from it, depending upon our state of faith.

When you are feeling ill, plagued by problems, your income
short, or a controversy arisen, where do you turn first in consciousness? Do you turn to the wellspring, or do you turn to
outer conditions and manifestations? I don't mean that we ignore that we have to be good stewards—certainly, we do. We
have to use our knowledge. But do we make *our knowlege of the
world* First Cause, or do we make *our knowledge of what we are
an expression of*—the I Am, the wellspring—First Cause? Do we
turn to the Omnipresence, or do we turn to already existing impressions when we have problems? This will tell us much concerning whether our will is keeping us from the wellsprings of
perfect expression.

ENJOY THE WELLSPRING
WITHOUT LIMIT

AS JOB STATED, "How much less to him that accepteth
not the persons of princes, nor regardeth the rich more than the
poor? for they are all the work of His hands." We are all one, and
the Father provides equally for each of us. Obviously, then, the
disparity comes because of consciousness. There is no mysterious God handing out "goodies" to one group and "baddies" to
another. Many of us feel there is. The wellspring is there for all
of us to enjoy equally and without limit; it is our understanding of what we are, of what we are a part of, that allows us to
partake as we will. Again, the will—the belief system—is the
control factor.

Most of the world have become idolaters and breakers of

at least one of the Ten Commandments. We often ignore the commandment, "Thou shalt not bear false witness against thy neighbor." Whenever we hold that God plays favorites, that "Lady Luck" is or is not on our side; when we envy or are jealous, conceited, or bigoted; and especially when we deny the I Am Presence in ourselves and in all others, we have broken the commandment of bearing false witness. We should keep, above all others, the First Commandment. "Thou shalt have no other gods before me," for, naturally, if we kept it, all the other commandments would take care of themselves. This is a perfect law. When we have no other authorities (which are gods), we immediately have opened the gates to our wellspring, and our will becomes submerged in God's will.

OPEN YOUR CONSCIOUSNESS

WE MUST REALIZE that God works to preserve all parts of His creation. God never lost anything. Nothing is lost in Spirit. Scientists tell us that the amount of energy in our world today is exactly the same as it was in the day of creation; only the manifested form is different. But God *does* allow us free will to accept or not accept the preservation. There is no arguing the fact that what God creates God preserves. But do we accept it? When anything goes wrong anyplace in God's world, there has not been Truth in that part of the world. God created all in perfection. He gave us a wellspring to bring about that understanding of the perfection that was in creation. If perfection is not there now, it is because of the absence of the Omnipresence *in our consciousness*; we have closed the gates of our wellspring.

The scientists, especially those who are spiritually endowed, in speaking of the quarks and other minuscule parts of the atom, tell us there is only oneness—just one Presence and Power. We are the ones who mold and condition these seemingly different parts of the atom ("Adam"). When we can open our consciousness to the fact that there is one Power and one Presence, we can become one with the consciousness of Solomon in Proverbs 16:22: "Understanding is the wellspring of life unto him that hath it." We all have it. We all have God's purity available to us, but we will not find our answers by looking to what has already been uncovered or discovered. We are not to ignore the knowledge of the world but to lift it up to come into what we call spiritual scientific understanding—lifting up to recognize that all is there in perfection. The abundance is there. With the understanding and acceptance of the Omnipresence and the purity of God's will, we are immersed in the abundant wellspring of all creation.

Ponder this marvelous statement by Herman Hedgedon in his book *The Bomb That Fell on America*: "Man without God is a bubble in the sea. A single grain of sand on an infinite beach. God without man is a mind without tongue, or ears, or eyes, or fingers, or feet. God and man together: we are such power as not all the atoms in all of creation can match!"

Is This All There Is?

IT IS DOUBTFUL IF there is an individual alive who has not said or thought, "Is this all there is?" concerning his or her life. We have thought about this "limitedness" in regard to our present life and circumstances and in regard to what we recognize as physical death. Particularly when we have loved-ones who make the transition to what we call death, we ponder, "Is this all there is to his or her life?" We sometimes ponder the departure of the physical body and often say, "He had such a full life," "She was cut down at the height of her ability," or, "How futile her life seemed." Frequently, we say to ourselves, "Life is so futile." Carried to the "nth" degree, sometimes we even contemplate suicide—we see no way out of a dilemma and no challenges and opportunities in the future. We, then, have often thought, "Is this all there is to life?"

WE ARE EXPRESSIONS
OF THE INFINITE

DESPAIR, A FEELING of a lack of any "meaningfulness" in life, stems from one primary cause: lack of identity of the individual as an expression of the Infinite. This lack results in feelings of frustration, limitation, and futility: all the real "demons" spoken of in the Bible. The only demonic force is created through the denial of the I AMness in the individual. Sin—releasing of the demonic force—ultimately can be traced to a denial of the Presence of God in the individual. This is good psychology, too, as it is a lack of an effective, realistic self-image that is at the root of psychological problems. The greatest of all "sins" and the greatest of all causes of despair and hopelessness is the same: lack of awareness of what the individual is in Truth. Hence, if there is a feeling of "Is this all there is?" it is due to the inability to truly relate to the Presence within—failure to recognize that what is in appearance is not the truth of what is.

There are many biblical expressions that can help us to understand our true nature and overcome this feeling of "helplessness" and/or futility. One of the greatest is "Seek ye first the kingdom of God and all else shall be brought unto you." Another, also from Jesus, is one of the very important Beatitudes: "Blessed are those who hunger and thirst after righteousness for they shall be filled." Once again from Jesus: "Truly, truly I say to you, before Abraham was, I am."

THE TWO TYPES OF DEATH

PAUL SAID THAT the last enemy to be overcome is death. There are two types of death and they are both the result of faulty understanding of the nature of man. One is the principal biblical meaning of death, and it has nothing to do with the body's ceasing to function. It is being "dead" to new concepts, "dead" to new ideas, "dead" to possibilities in living, "dead" to the potential for beauty, health, work, plenty, and joy. Many of our so-called living are truly the "walking dead" (zombies). Then there is what we know as bodily death—when the life forces no longer function. Paul, in his saying that the last enemy to be overcome is death, is speaking of *both* types. This is verified in much of his later work, especially the letter to the Corinthians wherein he explains the great meaning of love.

THE REALIZATION OF THE *I AM*

HOW DOES ONE have a resurrection in regard to the death that is identified as the "deadened mind"? It is achieved through the realization of what I Am—one with the Infinite. We can never help people overcome seeming problems in life until they realize that they have the potential to overcome them. Interestingly, we often use the word *handicap* to describe individuals who have physical and/or mental problems which limit them in their movement and in their thinking. Interestingly, the word *handicap* suggests the placing of a *cap* (lid or stopper) on the hand—which is the symbol of our ability to create, to bring forth new dimension. The Latin word for *hand* is *manus*, and it is from *manus* that we develop the words now commonly used as manufacture, manifest, manifold, etc. *Handicap* would mean, then, to place a cap on our uniqueness—Oneness with the Infinite. Most of us feel depressed, that life is futile, because we have handicapped ourselves through deadening our awareness of what we are. Life becomes a joy when the "cap" is removed and the great contents (potentials) are released. It is just as in opening a jar of jelly—we cannot get to the good part until we remove the lid, the cap.

In 1513 Fra Giovanni wrote a letter in which we find these

words of wisdom: "Life is so generous a giver, but we, judging its gifts by their covering, cast them away as ugly or heavy or hard. Remove the covering and you will find beneath it a living splendour, woven of love, by wisdom, with power." How often have we looked at things as they seemed to be and let ourselves become oppressed, discouraged, or miserable? How often in retrospection have we found these were but the stepping stones to greater joy and happiness than we had ever experienced before? *Look anew and life takes on life!*

MOVING INTO A NEW DIMENSION

As TIME (as man measures time) passes, there comes a point when the physical body can no longer contain the spirit which we are—it is then that the *real* self moves into a new dimension. Our spirit has to leave the limitation that the body has placed upon us. Truly, there is the time when "the spirit must soar" beyond form. This, of course, we in our ignorance call death. Actually, it is freeing the spirit from the handicap which the body has become. We have never learned—with some exceptions—that eventually the body has to be left in order for the spirit to express itself at a greater level.

Subconsciously, I suspect, the spirit, which man is, knows when it is time to move from the body into the pure spirit (God's ultimate paradise). Just as the spirit moved into physical attributes and physical limitations at birth, a time comes when the spirit knows it must leave the restrictions of the physical. It is simply moving into another dimension of life, which is what our destiny truly is: moving from glory to glory, from growth to greater growth.

Medically, death is the stopping of the vital functions of the organism; it is the organization (the matter) which ceases to have life. The Divine Plan behind the organization lives. All organizations require a plan; because the organism dies does not mean the plan is dead. "Death is a dark shadow of man's fear." The "dark shadow" is removed when we recall what we are in Truth.

Science has demonstrated that matter is never permanent and cannot be. It is in constant flux, constant change. There is no Substance there. However, Substance is permanent, never changing, ever consant. Personality is of matter, as is the body; the *real* self is of Substance (Spirit) and forever ("Before Abraham was, I Am").

Science tells us that energy never dies—only changes form. The Omnipresence (God) is all Presence, all-encompassing, which means it does not just include matter—it is all pervasive.

Energy is always moving into another form, and it always makes that "formation" based on the qualities it has been attracting in the previous form. Biblically, it is explained through this passage: "Till heaven and earth pass, one jot or one tittle shall in no wise pass from the law, till all be fulfilled." We are accumulating, through what we do and through what we give our attention, the energies which will move as spirit into the next dimensions. Our rewards are being accumulated right now—and our demerits. You are, as the medical world calls it, electromagnetic; thoughts and actions are your magnetic poles. So this statement, to which all seem to give voice, is absolutely true: "As a man thinketh in his heart, so is he."

Every form there is—whether we call it a life or an inanimate object—is constantly changing, constantly emerging into a new formation based on the accumulation through attraction. Our mind is the great agent for attraction: our "thought world" is the key to our magnetism.

We all have to graduate—we all have to come into new experiences in order to grow. Death is a graduation into another level (grade) of understanding—all that can be. Would you stop a child from graduating from grammar school because you loved her so much you didn't want to see her leave? Would you feel your presence was more important than her growth in knowledge and wisdom?

It is only our human mind that thinks, "This person is dead."

Words from scripture that are helpful, too, state, "In my Father's house are many mansions (dimensions)" and "I go to prepare the way." The I Am of our own consciousness is always preparing the way—our thoughts and attitudes are always preparing the way. We move into the next dimension of life at the level and in the manner in which our concepts of our own being prepared the way. Again, energy can come into form only through the attributes it has been attracting—that which is of its nature.

UPWARD AND ONWARD

IT IS HELPFUL to realize that the Infinite's Will—the Will of God (Law)—is always for movement upward and onward —never backward, never punishment, never limitation. We have pledged "Thy will be done." As the "executor" of that Will, we must attempt to live within God's Law or we cannot be an effective executor of Spirit's Will.

We must cease thinking of life and death as being separate— we must not think of "here" and "there." We must learn to concentrate on eternal verities, as difficult as that is. Life is eternally *now*! It always has been and always will be.

Time and space are strictly concepts of limited consciousness. Both time and space are man-made ideas. In Divine Mind there is no such thing as time and no reality to space. There is *no* emptiness. We must remember that mortality (the physical) is *not* immortality and never can be.

As difficult as it seems, it must be realized that the physical body must cease to function at some point in order for what we truly are (Spirit) to grow and to experience new dimensions of life. I believe that we enter into a dimension where we experience no burdens of economic pressure and we are employed in work which is pure joy and growth. We move into a dimension where there are no "dead-lines," no rush, and where the growth of the knowledge of Spirit is unlimited. Truly, we must experience what we call death in order to experience totally the life of Spirit. Paul stated that we put on the "mantle of immortality."

We must forever keep in mind and heart that the Will of God is ever "upward and onward" and that death is a movement upward into greater and greater awareness of Truth.

TURN TO THE *I AM*

THE VERY PURPOSE of our creation is unfoldment, growth. The essence of our life is spirit. Spirit teaches us this: I live; I am eternal; there is no death—there are only changing experiences.

There is no question that we all feel physical losses, and the only manner in which we overcome is the recognition of the "good," "God," coming forth through the change. We find comfort in the recognition that God is helping and directing.

"That life in Truth is ever Lord of death, and love can never lose its own." When we feel "dead" in our daily living and in regard to the physical separation from a loved one, we should turn our attention to what we are: what I Am. Come back home again.

LIFE WITHOUT BEGINNING OR END

GOD (SPIRIT) IS not only Love; God is also Life—Life without beginning or end—from everlasting to everlasting. Could you conceive of a thought of death being brought into life? No. Then God is not the author of anything that He is not Himself. In Ezekiel we are told that He wills not the death of any but that all should come to Him and love.

Death is the absence of the life idea from the body consciousness; when the life idea is withdrawn, the body is abandoned to corruption. In Romans 5:12 and 5:19, it is written that through disobedience sin entered into the world, and death by sin. In the second and third chapters of Genesis, we see that the disobedience was in eating of the tree of knowledge of good and evil—in other words, believing in a power of evil as well as good, thus setting up a false god and attributing a part of the One Power (God) to evil.

God is Good, Life, Love, Substance, Power, Strength, Intelligence. He is Spirit—Mind. Only God and His qualities are real and abiding; and it was and is His will that we should gain all of our experiences through the good, thus avoiding inharmonies. He made us, however, with a will to choose for ourself; and we chose to believe the serpent, or to look to the outer for guidance, thus believing the lie that we must know and experience evil as well as good to become like God. When we partook of evil in mind, we at once separated ourself in consciousness from our Parent, from Life, Love, Intelligence—and from that time on, we were dead in trespass and sin. What we call death is simply the culmination of belief in evil, the separation from God, in a dissolution of Spirit, soul, and body.

RECOGNIZE THE ONE POWER

EVERY SEEMING EVIL that manifests itself in our world comes directly or indirectly from the thought of being something separate, or apart from God, from a belief in evil as power instead of the recognition of the One Power, One Presence, the Good, the Omnipotent. Today, there is even a widespread race belief that God is the author of sickness and death, that He sends them upon people. This is unrighteousness and causes many to suffer from things when, in other ways, they seem to live righteous lives.

THE MEANING OF LIFE

JESUS GAVE US the perfect way to revolve into perfect living—to find meaning in life and to know "this is *not* all there is." He did this through the Beatitudes. The Beatitudes are states of consciousness—thought forms that allow us to live in perfect harmony with all of the outer world and to find the inner peace that passes all understanding. Through the practice of the Presence of God Within—which is the purpose of the Beatitudes—we move into the self we were intended to be: perfect expressions of the I Am, perfect expressions of God. As Jesus said, "For this I was born." It is for this that we are all born. That is the meaning of life, and that is *all there is*: to make manifest the Presence of God (the Whole—"holy"—Spirit). Yes, we were born to more perfectly express God. We were born in order for God to manifest Himself in flesh—to give expression to the Divine Idea (plan). The "plan" is the purpose of our birth.

Think of how Jesus recognized a purpose—meaning—for existence: as a boy of twelve, he insisted, "I must be about my Father's business." As a man, he declared, "I must work the works of him who sent me." To his disciples he said, "I am among you as one who serves." With his last breath, he sighed, "It is finished."

What Jesus said of himself, we must say for ourselves: We are here for a purpose, we must be about our Father's business, we must work while it is day, we are among others as those who serve, and for this we have come into the world.

We are not all here to teach or preach, but we are all here, as God gives us strength, to love, to help lift the world, to bring the Christ consciousness to humankind, and to aid in bringing in the Kingdom of God.

As William L. Sullivan, M.D., states, "I am a moral personality under orders."

Yes, there is much more to us than meets the eye. There is more to life than we can even begin to comprehend, and there is no death beyond that of the physical. As Walt Whitman said, "You are not all included between your hat and your boots." We are here to make the trumpets sound even though we may not know it.

ACCEPT THE GIFT

THE INFINITE DOES not fill heaven and earth with anything but pure Substance—and God gives man dominion over that Substance. Our awareness and acceptance of this Substance is entirely up to our own free will. If our lives feel "empty" and "lacking in meaning" we should remember that all of us belong to one family, and all possess in potential the same powers and possibilities as were manifested by Jesus and others. God is no respecter of persons. His Substance is given to us equally—but as receivers of His good we have to accept the gift. The Substance is there, but we have to become attuned to it (called "atonement")—just as with the beams of a television or radio station. They are there but must be turned on and tuned in in order to be received.

"Turn on" and "tune in" to your real nature—one with the Infinite, an expression of the Creative Force and Power in the Universe—and your life will take on new meaning, new dimension, new understanding. Then, instead of saying, "Is this all there is?" you will shout with joy, "There is more good here than I ever dreamed there could be!"

We are one with the Cosmos and we are one with the Creator, and there is far more for us in joy, enrichment, and fulfillment than has been "dreamt of in our philosophies."

How to Increase Your Equity for Life

WOULD YOU LIKE TO HAVE more control over your affairs, your work, your relationships? Would you like to feel as though you "owned" your own destiny? Obviously, the answer would be a resounding "yes." Your equity, ownership, of your "world" can be increased, and increased permanently!

The word *equity* is derived from the same basic Latin as *equal*. Until recently, equity meant the quality of being fair and impartial. In our time, it has come forward more in the meaning of *ownership rights*—derived from stockholders' versus bondholders' rights in corporations.

Actually, we think of *equity* today as the power of ownership. It has much the same meaning as *leverage*. In the financial marketplace, *equity* and *leverage* are used as almost synonymous terms and are given great weight—i.e., share of ownership.

Our concept of *ownership* is the source of our power—the concept, not the physical form.

Leverage is the increased power for action: Leverage always is gained by having weight on the side where we wish to apply pressure. This is a basic law of physics, and the Law of Leverage is a law of physics—the heavier weight will always have the power, the force.

In our lives, *belief* is the only leverage we have, but it is the only leverage needed because it is all-encompassing. It is all-encompassing because *encompassing* means to cover all points around: north, south, east, and west.

UNDERSTANDING THE NATURE OF GOD

Principle is the all-encompassing, complete leverage needed to demonstrate prosperity in all ways of life. Understanding the nature of God in man is Principle—accepting that there is One Law, One Mind, One Power, One Source. The author of Proverbs put it well when he said: "In all thy getting get understanding." He was speaking of Principle: One Cause, One Source, no divisiveness. St. Augustine said seventeen centuries ago, "The nature of God is as a circle whose center is everywhere, and its circumference nowhere."

The equity—leverage—is present everywhere and it has no limit, but it requires recognition. We must learn to recognize that the creation is over and is now waiting for the creative process in ourselves to make the revelation (Romans 8:19 RSV: "The creation waits with eager longing for the revealing of the sons of God").

EXPANDING OUR VISION

I DO NOT believe it is accidental that the Book of Revelation is singular: *Revelation*. When we come into the *revelation* that we are expressions of God, then all revelations become possible. When we expand our vision concerning what we are—expressions of God (image of God)—we then have the leverage (equity) to provide the security to make the many revelations which are our natural inheritance.

We have passed through fire light, candle light, oil light, gas light, and electric light, and are now involved with the laser, which is light amplification. It is cohesive light—concentrated—all working toward one goal and one objective. It is *centered*. It is the nuclei of energy. There are dimensions beyond the laser, but to have the ability to make the revelations that are there requires an expanded concept of what we are: the I Am.

We gain equity every time we expand the scope of our thinking in regard to our nature: expressions of God. We must remember that the word *scope* (vision) is the basis of the word *cope*. Whether we make it or not (whether we have the equity to overcome) depends upon our vision of what we *are* in Truth.

We did not unlock the secrets of the atom until we expanded our physical vision, which we did through the micro*scope*, nor did we unlock the secrets of the heavens until we went beyond our physical vision, which we did through the tele*scope*. In other words, we gained new equity—new understanding—by changing our *scope* (vision) through the micro*scope* and the tele*scope*.

EXPANDING EQUITY

So, TOO, IF we are to expand our equity (gain control), we must apply our awareness to our real nature: come into a "truth*scope*." Through the understanding of the Truth of our being, we shall have the *scope* (vision, equity) necessary to *cope* with all of the vicissitudes, problems, and seeming obstacles in our life.

Equity is built through expanded awareness, and the awareness which is of vital importance is that of our nature. There is not a single basic religion in the world, nor is there a psychologist or psychiatrist, who does not work on a basic premise: "What does the individual hold in regard to his or her true nature?"

Too often we are caught up in personality concepts. After all, personality concepts have to be limited. *Personality* comes from *persona*, which means mask. The mask that we wear is too often the mask of outer manifestations, which are fluid, and there is no substance in us.

RECOGNIZE THE *I AM*

How do we lose *equity*—the power to overcome? It is usually done by accepting "mastership" by outer conditions and events: experience, education, environment. As Lewis Carroll wrote in *Through the Looking-Glass and What Alice Found There*, " 'The question is,' said Alice, 'whether you can make words mean so many different things.' 'The question is,' said Humpty Dumpty, 'which is to be master—that is all.' "

What is "master" in our life? Is it recognition of what I Am, or is it the acceptance of limitation, disease, death, government (government as the source of our good), guilt, fear, and condemnation? Do we know our *intrinsic nature*? What we believe concerning our *intrinsic nature* determines our equity.

Are we intimidated by outer conditions—the limitations of the world (the *carnal mind*, as the Bible calls it)? The word *intimidation* tells us a great deal: *in-timid-ation* or *timid within*. This is the absence of the awareness of the I Am Presence. We can never rid the world of the limited idea—it is always available to us. (As Jesus put it, "The poor will always be with you.") However, we can change its form. Control over the limited idea comes when there is an awareness of the I Am and of what I Am a part. In the master teacher Jesus' words, "I come not to be ministered unto, but to minister" (Mark 10:45).

Are we allowing ourselves to be intimidated (ministered unto) by outer conditions? Have we lost our equity? We regain control by coming into an awareness of what we are. We overcome submission by having a new mission—a re-mission (new objective, new belief). As is stated in Romans 6:16:

> You know well enough that if you put yourselves at the disposal of a master, to obey him, you are slaves of the master whom you obey; and this is true whether you serve sin, with death as its result; or obedience, with righteousness as its result.

SURRENDER VENGEANCE TO INFINITE MIND

ONE OF OUR greatest problems in establishing a meaningful equity in and for life is a feeling of a personal need for competing and to "get even" for slights, wrongs, and injustices. One of the greatest of all equity "builders" is found in Psalm 94:1: "O Lord God, to whom vengeance belongeth; O God to whom vengeance belongeth." Similar words are to be found in Deuteronomy 32:35, Hebrews 10:30, and Isaiah 63:4. These scriptural passages are giving us a sound psychological principle: When vengeance is in the heart and mind, this becomes the goal—the striving. It is entirely negative, and through the practice of vengeance we lose equity.

We cannot expect to receive our glory (equity)—grow in consciousness—when centering on the concept of vengeance.

We cannot hold two thoughts in consciousness at the same time; hence, turn it over to God. Vengeance—the retribution (re-tribute)—is with Him. His Principle will prevail when we declare, "Divine right action *is* established in my mind." The Infinite Mind will provide for whatever *re-tribution* is needed.

Jesus asked, "What is this to thee?" Through understanding that the condition will be correctly adjudicated through the Infinite Mind, we get back into control of our own life. We should have no concern with getting even, sitting in judgment, competing for special recognition. It is all being handled very nicely. "Thank you, Father."

Isn't it wonderful that all concerns in regard to competition or compensation, or even vengeance, are now abolished, as they are now in perfect hands? What a freeing concept!

MOVE INTO A NEW DIMENSION

When we learn to let go of recompense, retribution, and vengeance, we free ourselves to move into another dimension. Newton's Third Law states, "For every action there is a reaction." The most important *actions* are those of the mind—attitude, the thought realm—and these can be mastered. We don't have to lose our equity to conditions, things, and events that are occurring in our world. In our mind, we do not have to react—through the mind we move beyond the laws of physics, including Newton's Third Law.

We should realize that *life is sequential.* Events—happenings—follow the sequence of our thinking. It was Job who stated, "What I greatly feared has come upon me." This is always an accurate statement. When you *fear* anything, you are cultivating that very thing and you have surrendered your equity to it. It is fear of the past that makes the future frightening. All-important to us is *visioning,* which is done through the mind.

We must learn to *vision* by magnifying the nature of God within our own being—expand the scope of our thinking in regard to the I Am.

Nothing is gained by going back to the past, looking on limitation, disease, poverty, vengeance. We merely cultivate the very nature of those things when we do. Expand the "truthscope" (see the Great Presence within yourself). Recent reports from the University of Texas and University of Michigan medical centers have proven that through positive visioning of overcoming a disease, the chances of recovery change dramatically for the better. We must learn to expand our vision of what we are, and we will have our healing: We will gain equity over the situation, as we will now have leverage.

ESTABLISH YOUR DOMINION

As JESUS SAID, "Pick up your cross and follow me" (*me* meaning the I Am Presence). Our cross is our ability to push aside (negate) all of the worldly appearances of limitation—cross them off. There are many stations along life's highway (stations of the cross), but at each station it is necessary to lift consciousness to the understanding that "I am God's beloved expression" —then the station is *moved over* (overcome). We have established our dominion, and we will rise to our final resurrection over all conditions and circumstances: Our equity is on a firm foundation. We are no longer ministered unto, but we are the minister. We become master of all we survey. We have *dominion* within us—we have the leverage within, no matter what the outer may pronounce. When we change our vision of our own identity, the world *for us* will change.

As Jean Cocteau wrote, "I am here to make the trumpets sound." We are here to call for the *glory* (the *glow-ray*) which is our inheritance as children of God—His perfect expressions.

Are You Having an Inquisition?

PERHAPS THIS ESSAY SHOULD be entitled "Are You Having an Audit?" rather than "Are You Having an Inquisition?" Actually, an inquisition *is* an audit, but usually predicated on prejudice and judgment. An audit is normally a listing of assets and liabilities and seeing if they are correctly reported. Like it or not, all of us are going through a type of audit called an inquisiton constantly. We are always inquiring about the state of our financial, physical, and mental health. We keep questioning these aspects of our lives and attempting to bring them up to whatever we consider "good." How many times we hold the inquiry based on prejudice and preconceived notions of what is good and what is bad! We are attempting to "eat of the tree of knowledge of good or evil." And, of course, each of us "dies" at the level of our belief concerning these conditions.

131

SEEK TRUTH WITHIN

NATURALLY, THE WORD *inquisition* is based upon another word, *inquire*. *Inquire* comes from the Latin *inquirere* —*in* and *quaerere*, meaning to seek. Hence, if used correctly, it is *to seek answers from within*. It can be the highest of all understanding: to seek Truth within and not from the sense world. As with any great asset, it can be greatly misused. All of us are familiar, at least slightly, with the Inquisition of the Middle Ages—particularly the Spanish Inquisition, which was a horror beyond description. The original court of Inquisition was established in the twelfth century by Father Dominic, who was charged by Pope Innocent III to excite Catholic princes and people to extirpate heretics. Later, punishment of heretics became a part of the inquisition. Very soon after the Catholic Inquisition was established, it became a method of weeding out any dissenters to the dogma, creed, and mandates of the leaders of the Church, many of whom were strong political leaders, especially in Spain.

HISTORY OF *INQUISITION*

FOR THE READERS interested in a more in-depth explanation of *inquisition*, I would refer them to Joseph T. Shipley's *The Origin of English Words* (Johns Hopkins Press, 1984). Dr. Shipley has done an outstanding piece of work of explaining various aspects of the Latin *quaerere* and how it became the basis— with various prefixes—of such words as *quest, question, query, acquire, conquest, inquest, inquisition*, etc. He states that *the* Inquisition was generally administered by the Dominicans and that it was begun around 1210 and lasted in France until 1772 and in Spain, where Queen Isabella and Tomás de Torquemada gave it a great impetus aimed mainly at Jews and Arabs, until 1838.

It is most interesting that the Inquisition was originally designed to measure the sincerity of new recruits to Catholicism. It was also intended to be a test of faith, of one's acceptance of God Within. As we know, it soon became a kind of witch-hunt and a test of faith in only one particular dogma. When one tries to test the faith of another, there ordinarily follows some kind of "witch-hunt," which is disastrous to all concerned.

WHAT IS OUR FAITH
AND UNDERSTANDING?

THE REASON FOR briefly summarizing the story of the Church Inquisition is to point out that whenever man judges the faith of others and their "use" of the faith, he is in trouble. "Judgment is mine, saith the Lord" is a great Truth. We certainly witnessed this recently in regard to so many of our evangelical television church leaders. We must not rejoice over this "circus" that transpired, but we can learn great lessons from it. The lesson above all else is simply this: Never judge the faith and understanding of others. This is not our job or our responsibility. Our job is this: Have I helped others to lift their consciousness above form and into the realization that within them is the power and the glory? And, above all: What is my own faith and understanding?

Many years ago, the great philosopher and teacher Immanuel Kant wrote, "If what I feel and know were felt and known by everyone, would the world be better off than it is right now?" (This is known as Kant's Categorical Imperative.) This is the question that we must ask of ourselves; this is the inquisition we must make. The really effective and meaningful inquisition is to ask of ourselves, and no one else: What do I believe within? The important inquisition is when we examine what we believe, what we hold true, what we hope for, and ask what this does for the betterment of mankind. Only we ourselves can hold this inquisition.

TRUE INQUISITIVENESS TAKES US BEYOND THE FIVE SENSES

Inquiry is the basis for our word *inquisitive*. What a great concept *inquisitive* brings to mind! It is the "parent" of curiosity, the progenitor to finding answers. Without inquisitiveness, we never venture beyond form, condition, and circumstance. It is the basis of all science and all inventiveness. How marvelous if this inquisitiveness could be brought forward into our thinking concerning what we are and of what we are a part! How "freeing" if it would be applied to examining our faith rather than looking at all things and conditions at so-called "face value"!

True inquisitiveness takes us beyond the five physical senses. If all were revealed to us through our physical senses, there would be no forward movement of humankind. There would be no imagination at work, and there would be no breakthroughs in knowledge of "what is." It is the very special part of childhood where we keep asking questions because we want to know—we are inquisitive. As Thomas Huxley wrote, "The secret of genius is to carry the spirit of the child into old age."

Imagination is the key to our moving into new dimensions; but for imagination to work there must be inquiry: Do we believe that we can understand, that it is good for us to understand, and that we can do it through applying this marvelous gift of imagination? Imagination, of course, is unique to humanity. As far as is known of the Universe we are the only creatures that can use imagination—but to use it effectively, a sense of curiosity, inquiry, is necessary. Also, as one becomes more aware through the inquiry as to what one is, one becomes more and more inspired. Imagination needs inspiration to do its good work. (Imagination without inspiration is what is known as worry.)

BUILDING "FAITH VALUE"

THE INQUISITION THAT we should be having is in regard to our "faith" values, not necessarily our "face" values. Building "faith value" requires using the imagination. The inquiry should concern what we believe and hold as Truth in our lives. We can certainly be aware of our financial condition through an examination of our checkbook and income and expense statements; we can receive a knowledge of our physical condition through a thorough medical examination; but it is only through personal inquiry that we can know our state of faith—our belief system. A personal inquisition is absolutely necessary. No priest, counselor, or psychiatrist can give us a complete rundown of our belief system; only a personal inquiry will do this, and it is a very healthy thing to do.

A biblical statement which applies quite aptly here is found in Ecclesiastes 7:10: "For thou dost not inquire wisely concerning this." When we hold the inquisition concerning only our physical and financial conditions, we are not inquiring wisely. Also, in Ecclesiastes 7:12, it says, "For wisdom is a defense, and money is a defense: but the excellency of knowledge is, that wisdom giveth life to them that have it." Knowledge of what we are in Truth is the result of our personal *inquisition*—being curious about what we are and allowing ourselves to move beyond what is known physically and through experience, education, and environment.

John Locke, the great philosopher and the philosopher for many of our nation's Founders, said, "The first inquiry of a rational being should be, who made me? the second, why was I made? who is my Creator and what is his will?"

RECOGNIZE THE ONE CAUSE

ASK YOURSELF: "Am I inquiring wisely into my affairs, my activities, and my understanding, or am I allowing my five physical senses to make my analysis?" Would it be said of your inquiry that "thou dost not inquire wisely concerning these activities"? Have you gone back to First Cause—One Presence and One Power in the Universe—or have you come to the inquisition with strong beliefs in limitation, separation, illness, poverty, lack, and depression?

Whatever we bring to the inquisition will be our *prejudice* in regard to the inquiry. The word *prejudice* is derived from *pre-judgment*. All of us come to any investigation with prejudice— some pre-judgment. However, there is only one prejudice which allows the inquiry to be wise, and that is the recognition of One Cause: One Presence and One Power. This is the ultimate and right *prejudice* for a creative inquisition: "I recognize that there is One Presence and One Power which is Cause, and there can be none other." If we recognize this One Presence as Cause (which we have identified as God), then all inquiries will be fruitful and will bring forth the right expression into our lives. This will fulfill the biblical admonition to be faithful to the God Presence—to trust in the Lord.

Many of us try to analyze all conditions and situations that come into our lives, and that, in itself, is all right. However, we begin the analysis with a false premise; therefore, the conclusion is bound to be either in error or limited. It is as in mathematics: One cannot have effective and correct results by beginning the calculations with an error. The laws of mathematics, which have so much certainty in them, are very applicable to our inquiries, our inquisitions. We must begin an inquiry on a sound basis. This means that we cannot begin an effective inquisition, analysis, calculation, without recognizing First Principle, First Cause.

We should remember that analysis always produces conclusions, but this does not mean that the analysis is synonymous with understanding. This is what John Locke meant when he said, ''The first inquiry of a rational being should be, who made me? the second, why was I made? who is my Creator and what is his will?'' If we have made these inquiries first, then future analyses and inquiries will be based on a proper premise and, above all else, on true understanding.

MOVE BEYOND THE FIVE SENSES

WE MUST NOT judge with our five physical senses—they will fool us frequently. Any judgment must be made first through an awareness of what we are: created by God in His image and likeness. Hence, all of the attributes of the Infinite are within us. This becomes our "rod and staff," as we all recognize from the mighty 23rd Psalm, "Thy rod and thy staff, they comfort me." This expression explains that the support is there with us (we even use the term *staff* in management and the military to indicate supporting individuals and activities), and the proper understanding will uphold us (a rod can be used to support and to fend off that which might attack the support).

The five physical senses are important in that we must use the good intelligence that has been gained through seeing, hearing, feeling, tasting, and smelling. These five senses have already revealed a great deal in the physical realm—but the five physical senses, used as a framework for a true inquisition, can reveal nothing that has not already been discovered. Through a true inquisition we should move beyond the framework of present limited understanding. Curiosity, in and of itself, is of little value unless we have the understanding that we can move beyond what is now known. So, too, with an inquiry—there must be a faith beyond the known.

The late Dr. Joseph Murphy said many times that we become what we contemplate. This is an absolute truth. Hence, when we are inquiring as to the truth of our being, we must first predicate our thinking and investigation on First Cause; then our contemplation, inquisiton, curiosity, will bring even greater strength to the Truth of what I Am. Everything is built on the premise of what I Am.

IMAGINATION WITH INSPIRATION

As STATED EARLIER, imagination is one of our great gifts, and the use of an inquiring mind is the first step in developing imagination. Naturally, the imagination requires a movement beyond the five physical senses; however, imagination must also have inspiration or it can take a nasty turn and become worry, depression, bleakness. The inspiration will be there when we attempt to use the imagination effectively if we have first established the framework of the Truth of what I Am: One with the Infinite. This is the necessary prejudice, predisposition, to make certain that the great gift of imagination is used in an effective manner; this will prevent us from "dying" to the seeming limitations in our lives; this is the protection which is promised biblically and accepted in psychology. The Book of Genesis states, "He who eats of the tree of knowledge of good or evil shall surely die." When we begin to inquire, analyze, and/or use our imagination, if we are of two minds (good/evil), we die to the true understanding and we become exiled from the answered prayer—we are out of the "Garden of Eden."

UNDERSTANDING AND FAITH

ONE OF THE greatest lessons given in regard to "holding the right thought or understanding" concerning any inquiry we may have is the story of Peter, the first disciple selected by Jesus. Peter's original name was Simon, and it was changed to Peter by Jesus. What a story is told through these two names! Simon means *hearing*, which means being receptive and discerning of Truth. Peter, or Cephas, means *rock* and signifies a faith in God that is strong, unwavering, and enduring. This faith, of course, is a necessary foundation for building spiritual consciousness in the individual. As Jesus said, "Upon this rock [Peter] I shall build my church."

All of us are building our churches on the rock which is our faith. We develop faith first through *hearing*—understanding the nature of what we are; then we are as a *rock*—we have a firm frame of reference (foundation). Whatever we have faith in is our foundation; it is that upon which we build our life, our church. Whatever we have faith in becomes the framework for all the answers we receive to our inquiries. We cannot escape the seeming trap which is faith. (I write *trap* even though this might seem an inappropriate term; but it snares everyone.) If our faith is in things, conditions, and circumstances rather than in the Truth of what I Am, the end results of all inquiries will be based on (limited to) things, conditions, and circumstances. A great inquisition would be just this: "What do I hold as the Truth concerning who I Am and what I Am?" When we find the answer with complete understanding, we will be free to judge the value of all things, and every inquiry will bring effective and uplifting results. As Jesus is quoted as saying in John 7:24, "Judge not according to appearance, but judge righteous judgment."

The concept of holding inquisitions has a very negative connotation in the minds of most people, and that negativity stems from awareness of the infamous Spanish Inquisition. This was not an honest inquisition, as it was predicated on a false premise: that some authority, official, can dictate the faith of others. We must realize that no one can dictate the faith of others. When we make a personal inquiry (a personal inquisition), we must be aware that we each build our own faith and that it must go beyond the opinions, concepts, and understanding of others or else the inquisition has been prejudiced from the beginning and is not valid.

THE WILL OF GOD

As was previously mentioned, John Locke wrote that among the first inquiries that must be made is "What is the will of the Creator?" How few of us *inquire* as to the Will of God even though we daily say, "Thy will be done" in the well-known Lord's Prayer (Prayer of Affirmation). How do we inquire —hold an inquisition—concerning God's Will? Can it even be done? Certainly it can be done, and it must be done. Is God's Will for illness, limitation, poverty, lack, depression, unhappiness? Is this the nature of the Universe? Or is the movement ever upward and onward? If we could fully understand that the Will of God is for plenty, health, joy, revelation, creation, and fulfillment, we would become free—free indeed. It is a belief based on a faulty analysis of God's Will that brings error into our world and creates the appearance of all of the negatives that are present in our society.

We must examine the perfection of the Universe—the preciseness of night and day, the seasons, the perfection of the heavens, the ability to imagine, to be inspired, to be intuitive—and we will begin to see the true Will of God. All of creation is evidence of the Creator. We know scientifically, as Albert Einstein stated, that matter (that which is visible to at least one of our senses) is energy reduced to the point of visibility. Behind all that our senses detect and all that lies behind those senses is Source. Behind every effect there is cause. We can realize this to some extent intellectually, but this understanding is not deep—it is rather shallow. As one of our greatest scientists has stated, "There is perfect order in the Universe, and man alone can understand that order."

Look to the *order* of the Universe and you will find the *Will of God*—perfect order to all life! The nonsense of belief in error —out-of-orderliness—serves no purpose except to make an effective inquiry into our very nature impossible. Subconsciously, through words, we have recognized that the Will of God is perfect order—this is why we say that when something is not performing as it was designed to do, it is *out of order*. We must inquire as to whether we are *out of order* with the Will of God and get ourselves into alignment with the Truth of our own being. We will then find that every inquisition we make will reveal ever greater treasures for us—that is the orderliness of the Universe. This is the ultimate revelation: Looking for order is looking for the Will of God!

DIVINE RIGHT ORDER
IS ESTABLISHED

SOME YEARS AGO in South Africa, a woman demanded —reallly *demanded*—that she speak with me after one of my lectures. I arranged to meet her the next morning, which is contrary to what I feel I can or should do when lecturing far from home. However, she was most persistent. I was grateful that I spoke with her, as she was a very interesting and "seeking" individual. She told me that since her husband had died some three years previously, her life had been one negative experience after another—loss of home, loss of the love of her two grown children, loss of her health. She said that she had tried to live a good life, always obeyed the Ten Commandments, and thought positively. She said she had asked herself over and over again, "Why me?" She added that she had been decreeing that all of these conditions in her life had come about because of some punishment she must have "earned" but she did not have the slightest knowledge of what she had done to "earn" these manifestations.

In speaking with her, I found that she was constantly holding a personal inquisition: "Why me? What have I done to bring these conditions about? Why don't my children love me?" She attempted to look for cause in the conditions. She had *prejudiced* the answer to her inquisitions so that there had to be negative results. She was looking outward for answers instead of inward —she was looking for cause in effect. She thought she was thinking positively by decreeing that she was an expression of the Infinite and that all good was open to her. But she was constantly inquiring as to the reason *why* conditions manifested which were very limiting.

I told her not to be so concerned with *why* these conditions happened to her and explained that every time she made an inquiry as to *why*, she was reinforcing in her subconscious the negative experience. As Jesus put it, "Let the dead [past] bury its dead." I told her that whenever one starts an inquisition with the desire to reveal why a negative condition took place, the subconscious will simply reinforce that negative condition; as "night follows day," the consequences in life will be more negative conditions.

I told her to inquire as to the Will of God and decree, "Divine right order is established in my mind, body, and affairs. Thank you, Father, for so it is" (a decree used, in part, by Unity co-founder Charles Fillmore). Look for the order in the Universe *now* and not for the disorder of old situations and conditions, because the revelation resulting from an inquiry depends upon the recognition and the understanding that the Will of the Universe is perfect order.

I am happy to report that two years later, when I returned to Pretoria, the woman told me that her life had changed dramatically. She said that she had been using the statement I had given her over and over again and that she started every inquiry concerning any conditions in her life with the statement, "Divine right order *is* established in my mind, body, and affairs. Thank you, Father, for so it is." The woman is now living a more productive life, has a magnificent new home, and is enjoying the presence of several lovely grandchildren. She had made the proper inquisition and found that there were no limitations possible with the Infinite, and that the Infinite was within her.

A MARVELOUS INQUISITION

WE MUST REALIZE that the world is a reactive organism —it does not act independently from our thinking. We must keep asking the great question embodied in Kant's Categorical Imperative: "If what I feel and know were felt and known by everyone, would the world be better off than it is right now?" What a marvelous inquisition, especially if coupled with John Locke's inquiry, "Who made me? why was I made? who is my Creator and what is his will?"

Have your inquisition. You will have it—like it or not. Take control and decree that all will be revealed to you just as the great promise made by Jesus states, "There is nothing covered, that shall not be revealed; and hid, that shall not be known [for those who believe]" (Matthew 10:26).

Love: The Scientific Evidence

WHAT A WONDERFUL AGE and time to be alive! So much of the hidden meaning of scripture—all scripture—can be verified through scientific work of the very highest nature. We are certainly privileged to live in this age because our faith no longer has to be placed on the words of others; now we can verify that our faith must be placed within, in the Omnipresence in ourselves—the ''secret place'' that Jesus discussed.

I believe that for our very survival on the earth we must comprehend the true meaning of love and must begin to practice the principles of the Christ. Certainly for centuries we have known through intuition and experience that through living by truth principles, through practicing the only rules ever laid down specifically by Jesus (the Great Commandment and the second like unto it), we lived a harmonious, joyful, and fruitful life. We did not, however, seem to have the scientific ability to prove to the

144

skeptic and to those who lived by mind alone (the so-called "intelligentsia") that the Great Commandment was important. Now this is no longer true.

WHAT MAN IS AND CAN BE

WHAT HAS HAPPENED in the past few years to make it possible for all of us to have unflinching faith and undying awareness of what we are and can be? There should be no one of reason alive today who does not understand the Omnipresence—the I Am Presence—which is always with us and available with unlimited supply for us. The word *unlimited* is meant quite literally. Let us examine a little of what science has found in respect to our true nature.

One of the greatest breakthroughs to understanding took place when we finally split the atom. It proved once and for all that eventually *all* matter was reduced to energy! The physical substance of humankind is eventually reduced to electromagnetic energy. All energy which has come into physical manifestation has within it electromagnetism. Hence, we, from our very essence, are electromagnetic!

But what is magnetism? Basically, for our purposes, we know that a magnet attracts to itself only that which it is. It cannot do otherwise—simply cannot. The molecules, the atoms, come into formation only because there are like particles. There is a repression and an expulsion and a resistance to non-like atoms. For this reason we can walk on cement and not have our shoes become a part of that cement—there is a different electromagnetic force at work in the cement than there is in our shoe leather. Atoms multiply through the attraction to like atoms and maintain their strength by adhering to that which they are. What a lesson for man!

THOUGHT ACTION

CLOSELY RELATED IS the knowledge we have gained through use of biofeedback techniques. In this country biofeedback has been revealed particularly by Dr. Elmer Green and his wife Alyce at the Menninger Foundation. It has been found that the primary energy force in us comes through thought action. We can prove today the effect that thought has on Alpha, Beta, Theta, and Omega waves within the brain. The great proverb "As he thinketh in his heart, so is he" can now be verified. The electromagnetic force which we are brings alive the magnetism dormant within us through the process of thought.

In my judgment, this is the great lesson of the story of Lot and his wife fleeing Sodom and Gomorrah, in which his wife looked over her shoulder and became a pillar of salt. To the ancients this was probably a very "real" story, as they knew salt as their only preservative. Today we know that salt is a form of crystal (solidified energy), and we know that energy which cannot express itself crystallizes. Hence, the lesson here, now verified by science, is that if we look on the past without love, and if we cannot look ahead for our good (love), we crystallize and become as Lot's wife—living pillars of crystallized energy, unable to move forward. We become unable to live a fruitful, abundant life because our electromagnetism now ceases to attract our good; rather, it now attracts only that which it is—the negative, the unloving.

LOVE IS PUREST THOUGHT

TODAY WE KNOW that we renew ourself physically every seven years. Then why, if we partake of only pure food, pure air, and pure water (which most of us do not) do we not become as new, ever young, and ever vital? The answer is simple and proved by science: The most important element of nourishment has not been brought into our physical being. That important element, of course, is pure thoughts. The purest form of thought is love. We have been holding on to the old, negative, unloving thoughts of ourselves, our neighbors, and our world. Dr. Shafica Karagulla, in her great work *Breakthrough to Creativity*, where she has used the various scientific devices better to understand health and disease, has found the following to be true:

> When an individual comes into the presence of a well-loved person, all three of his energy fields are intensely brightened. He appears to have more energy of a bright and scintillating quality in these fields. This is very apparent in comparison with his usual energy fields. A purely sex emotion appears to "muddy" the emotional field and dull the mental field.

Yes, there are three basic sides of man which must be developed—the body, the mind, and the spirit (energy). If any one of them is neglected—not treated with love—the renewal process will be imperfect, and we shall not come into the perfection of which we are capable. Again, thought lies at the bottom of the problem.

MAN'S UNLIMITED POTENTIAL

DR. HENDRIK WILLEMSZ of the Technical Institute of Amsterdam, in his book *The Great Secret*, points out that we have within our brain much greater power than the greatest laser yet built—in fact, unlimited potential. The whole principle of the laser is based on concentrated energy. Lasers today are capable of dissolving granite (changing its energy form) and of going through lead, etc. We could move mountains, as Jesus told us, if we brought our full energy into play—again, this is done through love. Probably, we could live forever in our physical form if all four elements were perfectly pure in our life—air, water, food, and thought. We would not, however, live in our physical form forever, because eventually we would reach the point where our purity would cause us to abandon the flesh— we would have accomplished all that could be accomplished on earth. We would become entirely etheric—matter would dissolve to pure energy, which is not physically visible.

BARRIERS TO OUR GROWTH

WEEK BY WEEK, month by month, in recent years, vast new discoveries are being uncovered which reveal our divine nature and the control we exercise over ourself and our world through the type of thoughts we hold. I would call to your attention these three articles of great importance: "Markers of Biological Individuality" (Scientific American, June 1972); "The Cartography of Meditation" (Science, November 26, 1971); and "The Physiology of Meditation" (Scientific American, February 1972). Of great importance, too, is Nigel Calder's The Mind of Man (Viking Press, 1971). These articles and this book are a few of many excellent scientific studies concerning humankind which can easily be related to basic scriptural writings. It just takes an opening of the mind—and the heart—to understand that our only real barrier to relating the truth in scripture and in science is one of prejudice and dogma. We must begin to understand that the barriers to our full growth in consciousness are those created through our thinking.

THE ELECTROMAGNETIC NATURE OF MAN

THE GREAT WONDER of our time—and probably the greatest wonder of all time—is the discovery of our electromagnetic nature. The wonder of magnetism! The proof of the truth of Christian principles is to be found in magnetism. Certainly, Jesus, who taught a simple message, a simple formula for living, recognized that it was through the placement of our thought that we grew, stood still, or retrogressed. One of the greatest of our American philosophers, Ralph Waldo Emerson, once said, "Never underestimate man's capacity for degradation or for exaltation." How right he was! He was correct because we have the capacity to bring anything to ourself through the tremendous magnetic power that we have. Wherever our thoughts are, there our affairs, our world, our very being, will be.

We live through what is often called "self-fulfilling prophecy." If we say that we are something other than a child of God, a part of the Omnipresence, then we are prophesying what we shall become, and what an accurate prophet we shall prove to be! We shall be accurate because we shall bring into our very being—our self-fulfillment—whatever has been in our consciousness. This is part of the law of magnetism.

LOVE SHOULD BE OUR CENTER MAGNET

LOVE, THE GREAT commandment, should be our center magnet. It must be the cornerstone of all that we do, because it is through love, and love alone, that we magnetize other individuals, good things, good thoughts, and abundance for ourselves. We become alive, magnetic, to whatever we concentrate on—good, indifferent, bad. If our concentration is on fear in any of its aspects, that is exactly what will come to us; we give it energy to come ever more abundantly into our life. If our commitment is to love—love without any "ifs," "ands" or "buts"— then we give energy to whatever is good for our well-being, and we bring it to ourselves. How beatifully Jesus gave us this message in the Great Commandment! How wonderful to have science verifying this fact for us!

WE CREATE OUR ENERGY FORCE

JUNGIAN PSYCHOLOGY, TOO, has verified the fact that whatever is in our consciousness becomes our fundamental "drive"—our spark and our fuel. We know that a habit cannot be changed by dwelling on the habit, but only by finding something else on which to concentrate. We are aware through psychology that our actual goals, our objectives, become that which is in the consciousness. Hence, if we are full of fear (the absence of faith in our own I Am Presence, Omnipresence), we have good reason to be fearful, because we are bringing into our world the very thing that we fear. Psychology tells us that this is so because the brain can hold in consciousness only one thought at a time, and that thought becomes a goal.

Now physics and allied sciences are demonstrating that we create energy force in ourselves which acts as a magnet to attract things, ideas, and concepts to ourselves through giving them our concentration. We become a powerful magnet for whatever receives our attention. Just as with magnets in the physical world which can attract to themselves only that which they are, so, too, with us. We bring alive our magnetic force through the thoughts that we hold; hence, we bring to ourselves the conditions, situations, ideas, and things to which we give our attention.